Whether a lifelong Bengals fan or a devoted follower of Jesus Christ, *Bengal Believer: 52 Who-Dey-Votions for the Cincinnati Faithful* strikes the perfect spiritual chord. Del Duduit once again blends together the perfect concoction of memorable football moments with soul-stirring Scripture. A joy to read. Who Dey!

—Dr. John Huang,
sports journalist and award-winning author, *Sports View America*

As a sports director at a southern Ohio radio station, I am on the go all the time. I love covering and broadcasting high school sports. There is nothing like the excitement along with the strong feeling and commitment to community. When I'm not watching local athletes compete, I am cheering on my Cincinnati Bengals. I'm a lifelong fan who has been there through the ups and downs. From dancing the "Ickey Shuffle" as an eleven-year-old in my parents' living room to seeing Joe Burrow guide the Bengals to Super Bowl LVI, I will continue to cheer on my guys in stripes. In this book, *Bengal Believer*, my friend and fellow sportscaster Del Duduit, takes me, and you, on a memorable journey for the Who-Dey faithful. He combines the history of great plays, players, and moments and uses them to inspire and encourage you. I'll be a loyal fan of the Bengals until the very end, and this book puts an exclamation point on why I bleed Orange and Black. Who-Dey for life.

—Chuck Greenslate, Sports Director, Hometown Broadcasting, WNXT Radio

Life isn't all fun and games and neither is football—a sport that requires discipline and hard work. Del Duduit has a knack for sharing lessons and inspirational anecdotes about the Bengals while expertly weaving in biblical principles that are applicable to life. Although I root for a rival team in Pittsburgh, *Bengal Believer* aims to prove that we all serve on "Team Jesus." Any sports fan will benefit from this thoughtful devotional.

—Beckie Lindsey, award-winning author and a fan of sports

I've covered the Bengals for decades for a newspaper in Cincinnati. I've also sat right next to Del Duduit in press boxes many of those years. We've shared many meals together and talked about the Bengals in the media dining hall with our colleagues for hours. We've covered the Bengals in the good and bad times. Most of the stories in *Bengal Believer* I know firsthand because I was there. I love how he tells the story behind the story and puts a life lesson in there for all of us to learn from.

—**Conrad Clowers,** sportswriter

I love *Bengal Believer*. I appreciate how Del blends in the stories from years past to today's NFL powerhouse team in Cincinnati. I cover the Bengals along with Del and have been through the bleak years and to a Super Bowl game with him in the press box. His accounts from crucial games to popular players along with spiritual life lessons makes this book a must on any bookshelf. Well done, Del.

—**Brendon Miller,** Blue Grass Sports Nation

More from Del Duduit

Stars of the Faith Series

Goal Line Devotions
Birdies, Bogeys & Blessings
Dugout Devotions II
First Down Devotions II
Dugout Devotions
First Down Devotions

Sports Shorts
Alabama Devotions
Auburn Devotions
Florida Devotions
Florida State Devotions

DEL DUDUIT

52 Who-Dey-Votions for the Cincinnati Faithful

BENGAL BELIEVER

Birmingham, Alabama

Bengal Believer

Iron Stream
An imprint of Iron Stream Media
100 Missionary Ridge
Birmingham, AL 35242
IronStreamMedia.com

Copyright © 2024 by Del Duduit

No part of this publication may be reproduced, stored in a retrieval system, or transmitted in any form or by any means—electronic, mechanical, photocopying, recording, or otherwise—without the prior written permission of the publisher.

Iron Stream Media serves its authors as they express their views, which may not express the views of the publisher.

Library of Congress Control Number: 2023950232

All Scripture quotations, unless otherwise indicated, are taken from the Holy Bible, New International Version®, NIV®. Copyright ©1973, 1978, 1984, 2011 by Biblica, Inc.™ Used by permission of Zondervan. All rights reserved worldwide. www.zondervan.com The "NIV" and "New International Version" are trademarks registered in the United States Patent and Trademark Office by Biblica, Inc.™

Scripture quotations unless otherwise noted are from the ESV® Bible (The Holy Bible, English Standard Version®), © 2001 by Crossway, a publishing ministry of Good News Publishers. Used by permission. All rights reserved. The ESV text may not be quoted in any publication made available to the public by a Creative Commons license. The ESV may not be translated in whole or in part into any other language.

Scripture quotations marked KJV are from The Authorized (King James) Version. Rights in the Authorized Version in the United Kingdom are vested in the Crown. Reproduced by permission of the Crown's patentee, Cambridge University Press

Scripture quotations marked NKJV are taken from the New King James Version®. Copyright © 1982 by Thomas Nelson. Used by permission. All rights reserved.

Scripture quotations marked (NLT) are taken from the Holy Bible, New Living Translation, copyright ©1996, 2004, 2015 by Tyndale House Foundation. Used by permission of Tyndale House Publishers, Carol Stream, Illinois 60188. All rights reserved.

Cover design by Jonathan Lewis / Jonlin Creative

ISBN: 978-1-56309-700-3 (paperback)
ISBN: 978-1-56309-701-0 (eBook)

1 2 3 4 5—28 27 26 25 24

This little book is dedicated to my granddaughter, Ember.

Although this was written and ready to go before you were born, I wanted to make sure it was for you. I know you will be a blessing to everyone around you and a treasure to me as well. I hope and pray we can have wonderful and fun times together, and maybe one day, I can take you to a Bengals game.

—Papaw

CONTENTS

Acknowledgments xi
Week 1: "You Don't Live in Cleveland!" 1
Week 2: Be a Record Breaker 5
Week 3: Make an Impact Play 9
Week 4: Pour It on the Enemy 13
Week 5: Leave No Doubt of Your Witness 16
Week 6: Be Dedicated to Your Team. 20
Week 7: Don't Waste Time 24
Week 8: Make the Most of Your Second Chance 28
Week 9: Come Through in the Clutch 32
Week 10: You Too Can Make a Comeback 36
Week 11: Become Inducted into God's Hall of Fame. . 40
Week 12: Play Like a Champion 44
Week 13: Celebrate Your Savior 48
Week 14: Be the Leader 52
Week 15: Overcome the Obstacles 56
Week 16: Encourage Others 60
Week 17: When Adversity Hits 64
Week 18: What Does Your Name Say About You? 68

Week 19: Where Is Your Courage?	72
Week 20: Prepare Your Family	75
Week 21: A Fresh Start	78
Week 22: Increase Your Spiritual Temperature	82
Week 23: Wait On Your Breakthrough Moment	86
Week 24: Keep Your Promises	90
Week 25: Be Steadfast in Your Journey	93
Week 26: Be Humble and Get the Job Done	96
Week 27: Establish and Enforce the Rules	99
Week 28: Bring Joy to Others	103
Week 29: Anticipate the Pass	107
Week 30: You Can Be Bold	111
Week 31: Stay on the Same Team	114
Week 32: Be Willing to Do What God Wants	118
Week 33: Don't Pay the Cost	121
Week 34: Be a True Friend	124
Week 35: Give Back to Your Community	127
Week 36: Kick the Enemy Through the Uprights	131
Week 37: Be a Valuable Member of God's Team	134
Week 38: Develop Your Skills and Talents	138
Week 39: What Does *Who Dey* Really Mean?	144
Week 40: Keep a Song in Your Heart	147
Week 41: Just Run Faster	150
Week 42: Set the Record	154
Week 43: The Phantom Call	157
Week 44: Reunited	160

Week 45: Do Your Best, No Matter the Outcome . . . 164
Week 46: No Refund Needed. 168
Week 47: The Comeback 172
Week 48: God Chose You. 176
Week 49: End the Streak and Go to the Super Bowl . 180
Week 50: The Baltimore Beatdown. 184
Week 51: Happy Birthday. 188
Week 52: God Will Give You a Second Chance. 192

ACKNOWLEDGMENTS

The following made this book possible. Thank you to:

My wife, Angie, for your help and encouragement.

My agent, Cyle Young, for your hard work and friendship.

My publisher, John Herring, for taking this book to the public.

My colleagues at the *Portsmouth Daily Times*—Paul Boggs and Hope Comer, for credentials to cover games.

My editors and production teams at Iron Stream Media—Michele Trumble, Susan Cornell, and Kim McCulla.

My Lord and Savior Jesus Christ for your blessings and forgiveness.

Week 1

"YOU DON'T LIVE IN CLEVELAND!"

A good person leaves an inheritance for their children's children, but a sinner's wealth is stored up for the righteous.
—Proverbs 13:22

The phrase is burned into the memories of every Bengals fan.

Sam Wyche was an iconic head coach in Cincinnati from 1984 to 1991. The black-and-orange faithful loved his spirit and enthusiasm. But on December 10, 1989, he became a legend.

The favored Bengals were predicted to blow out visiting Seattle and take charge in the AFC playoff picture. But this did not turn out to be the case.

Cincinnati struggled throughout the game, and in the third quarter, tensions came to a boil for Wyche. The Seahawks drove the ball near the end zone, and the crowd became restless and started to pelt the visiting players with snowballs. The officials gathered and discussed a possible penalty on the home team. The Seahawks stopped play while the fans tossed the snow.

Wyche, already frustrated with the officials, darted across the field and snatched the microphone from the public-address announcer. He was direct and to the point: "Will the next person who sees anybody throw anything on the field, point him out and get him out of here?" Wyche bellowed with a booming voice of authority. "You don't live in Cleveland, you live in Cincinnati!"

The home crowd roared in delight in support of Wyche's remarks, a direct hit to the Bengals' biggest rivals from about a four-hour drive northeast of the Queen City.

Cincinnati, however, lost the game 24-17 and failed to reach the playoffs. Although the fans were devastated that their high-powered offense did not make the post-season, they will forever love Wyche for the way he defended and loved his team with passion.

What legacy do you want to leave? How will your family and others remember you? Does one act or remark make you a legend or a disappointment?

> *The righteous lead blameless lives; blessed are their children after them.*
>
> —Proverbs 20:7

Huddle Up

Maybe you just finished college and landed a good job. Or you and your wife are new parents and want to give your children noteworthy memories. The ball is on your side of the field. There are no blockers in front—it's up to you to leave a positive legacy for others to follow.

Quick Snap

Once you make the decision to take responsibility for your reputation, here are some suggestions to follow to establish an impressive and fond heritage:

1. Encourage and inspire others: There is enough negativity in the world. Make the effort to be the exact opposite. Demonstrate joy throughout the day. In the third chapter of Hebrews, God gives wonderful advice: "Therefore encourage one another and build each other up, just as in fact you are doing" (1 Thessalonians 5:11).
2. Give your time and money: God promised to supply your needs. In turn, give back to the community and church. Become involved in charity work, and donate your time to worthy causes with an energetic attitude. Excel in grace and give back.
3. Demonstrate unconditional love: Show genuine affection for your family—even those who stray from the fold. You are not required to accept sin, but God does expect you to show love for the sinner. Be glad to see your loved ones and treasure each moment.
4. Forgive others: In the fourth chapter of Ephesians, you are instructed to be kind and compassionate and pardon those who have wronged you. This is a tough one to master, but you must put forth the effort. Forgiveness removes a burden from you and brings you peace and fulfillment. Grudges are heavy. Toss them off and rejoice, because God forgives your sins

too. "For if you forgive other people when they sin against you, your heavenly Father will also forgive you" (Matthew 6:14).
5. Live the example: When those around you notice your dedication to your family and church, it resonates with them as a bright witness. Play by the rules of God's Word at home and at work. Do your job and lead your loved ones.

You don't have to live in Cincinnati or Cleveland to be the example. You must choose to live a life of holiness in your house, and God must live in your heart. Take pride in your life and defend your values. Tell the devil he does not live in Cleveland, nor anywhere you call home. Who Dey!

Week 2

BE A RECORD BREAKER

Delight yourself in the Lord, and he will give you the desires of your heart. Commit your way to the Lord; trust in him, and he will act.

—Psalm 37:4–5 ESV

On October 22, 2000, Denver's "Orange Crush" defense strolled into Paul Brown Stadium on a mission. The Broncos had a 4-3 record while Cincinnati hoped to muster up an effort to garner its first win.

However, the NFL's second-best defense was no match for Bengals' running back Corey Dillon, as he shattered one of professional sports' "unbreakable" records. He tore apart the defense, rushed for 278 yards, and led Cincinnati to a 31-21 win over a stunned Denver squad. The tailback broke Walter Payton's twenty-three-year-old record of 275 yards rushing set against Minnesota.

Since then, Dillon's mark has been bested by Jerome Harrison of the Cleveland Browns (2009), Jamal Lewis of Baltimore (2009), and Adrian Peterson, who now holds the record of 296 yards rushing while he played for Minnesota in 2007.

But Dillon set the standard. He carried the ball twenty-two times for an average of 12.6 yards per carry. Keep in mind the Denver defense had given up an average of 64.7 yards rushed per game. When Payton set the record, he had forty-one carries while Dillon needed almost half of the totes.

The Bengals experienced quarterback issues at the time, so most defenses targeted their running game. Thus, when Dillon ripped through the Denver defense, he added insult to defeat.

When Cincinnati entered the contest, they had a goal to win the game. When the day ended, their accomplishment exceeded any expectations.

What goals do you have? What record will you establish?

He will bring forth your righteousness as the light, and your justice as the noonday. Be still before the Lord and wait patiently for him.

—Psalm 37:6–7 ESV

Huddle Up

You may not have goals. After all, they can be hard to set. You might pick one not so hard to reach at first, then you can settle your sights on a task less difficult. But, at the end of the day, you want to achieve a feat you can reflect back on with pride. Corey Dillon probably did not enter this particular day with the mindset to break Walter Payton's single game rushing record. But he did. He stayed focused and executed his job. Sometimes, this happens. Don't make goals too lofty to reach. And if you are not sure of your purpose, then wait for God to reveal it to you in His time.

Quick Snap

Perhaps you know what you want to accomplish. That's fantastic. But in case you are undecided, here are a few targets to ponder:

1. Never fall away from your faith. Be confident in what you believe. Understand and embrace your beliefs. In 1 Peter, we are told to be prepared to give an account to everyone who asks. Study the Word, and never back down.
2. Be open and honest. You might be faced with a question you don't know how to answer. Never fake the play. Instead, do what Corey Dillon did each day. Practice. Read God's Word every day, and set a goal to read through it at a steady pace. When you finish, start over again. This arms you when the tough questions come so you can slash through the defense and give the right answers.
3. Always put God first: God is pleased when you put Him and your family ahead of your own needs. Your own wants should seldom take precedence.
4. Demonstrate patience: You might want a favor now, but the Lord may make you wait. He knows best. Listen to your coach, and hang on for the right play to be called at the right time. Chances are, if you try to force results on your own, you may get blitzed and sacked for a loss.
5. Memorize scripture: When you run into a goal-line stand in life, the Bible can bring comfort, give you

a song in your heart, and fill you with wisdom to lead the charge. Find a few verses that hold special significance for you and commit them to memory. In Ephesians, we are told God's Word is the belt of truth—put it on and wear it with confidence.

Goals are hard to set and reach. But you must have a target to shoot for at some point. There is no timetable to set them, but the Lord reveals His plan to you when the time is right. He may just hold off for the best defense in the league to show up to play before he produces His game-winning offense with you at the helm. Be patient, and wait on the Lord. He will set the mark for you. Who Dey!

Week 3

MAKE AN IMPACT PLAY

And do not forget to do good and to share with others, for with such sacrifices God is pleased.

—Hebrews 13:16

The moment was all his. Stanford Jennings caught the kickoff and returned the ball 93 yards for a dramatic and much-needed touchdown with under a minute left in the third quarter of Super Bowl XXIII. The twenty-six-year-old put his Bengals ahead 13-6 over San Francisco with the second-ever kick return for a TD in Super Bowl history.

Jennings, a 1984 third-round draft pick out of Furman, found a crease in the defense and scampered the distance. For a little while that day, Cincinnati fans had hoped for their Bengals to win it all. But the fourth quarter featured a comeback for the ages.

The 49ers won the championship game 20-16.

But the punt returner, who became a father the night before when his wife, Kathy, gave birth to their daughter Kelsey back in Cincinnati, came through and delivered when his team needed him. He made a contribution and a difference.

What impact do you have on those around you? Are you prepared to make a big play?

Therefore encourage one another and build each other up, just as in fact you are doing.
—1 Thessalonians 5:11

Huddle Up

Do you want to get in the game of life and have an impact on society? Everyone does. But few people take action and make the big play. Perhaps you have been on the sidelines too long and are ready to make a difference. What can you do? Keep in mind, you do not have to set the world on fire. Strive to please the Lord and spread His love.

Quick Snap

The coach calls your play. You enter the game and want to make an instant impact. However, this stage does not include fanfare or accolades. You must succeed because you want to. Here are some plays you can make to contribute to the kingdom of Christ:

1. Visit your local hospital and read to sick children. This might take some organization and approval from the social services department, but the effort is worth it in the end.
2. Become involved in local politics. Find your political organization, attend meetings, and offer to help. The potential is endless. Who knows? You can even

run for office. Your neighborhood and county need principled individuals in positions of leadership. Christians are needed to serve in all levels of government—federal, state, county, and local.
3. Run for a seat on the board for your local school or youth sports organization. Don't sit back and let people you don't agree with run the show. Get off the bench and get into the game. Children need leaders who demonstrate character.
4. Volunteer for a civic organization close to your heart. Charity clubs such as the American Cancer Society or Right to Life organizations are always eager to welcome new faces. Become involved and stay dedicated to your commitment.
5. Be a Big Brother or Big Sister. Show determination and patience to a young child who needs guidance and stewardship. Youngsters remember those who helped them, and they are inspired to return the favor to others.
6. Organize a group of men to help provide a widow with lawn maintenance or needed repairs to her home.
7. Help clean up your neighborhood. When others see you take pride in where you live, they may join in to help you.
8. Lend a hand at a food pantry. Help those who are in need.
9. Make regular visits to a hospice unit and take donuts or snacks to the nurses who work there.
10. Pay for the meal of a person behind you in a drive-thru, and don't let anyone else know you did this.

You don't need thousands of people to cheer you on like Stanford Jennings on national television. He rose to the occasion and came through for his team. As a Christian, you can do the same and glorify Christ through good deeds. While works will not get you into heaven, they make your journey sweeter each day. Who Dey!

Week 4

POUR IT ON THE ENEMY

For though we live in this world, we do not wage war as the world does. The weapons we fight with are not the weapons of the world. On the contrary, they have divine power to demolish strongholds. We demolish arguments and every pretension that sets itself up against the knowledge of God, and we take captive every thought to make it obedient to Christ.

—2 Corinthians 10:3–5

In the fight for the human soul, good sportsmanship does not exist. Then there was December 17, 1989, in Cincinnati.

The Houston Oilers were in town, and Coach Jerry Glanville and Bengals coach Sam Wyche did not like each other. Their intense rivalry did not allow for any exchange of Christmas cards, hugs, or kisses. In fact, they didn't even shake hands.

Bengals quarterback Boomer Esiason enjoyed a tremendous day. He threw for 326 yards and four touchdowns, and he completed twenty of his twenty-seven pass attempts. From the first possession, Cincinnati meant business, and they scored on their first four drives to post a 28-0 lead.

When the game ended, the Bengals had crushed Houston 61-7.

To add insult to defeat, Cincinnati kicked a field goal with twenty seconds left in the game instead of taking a knee to secure the win. But Wyche wanted to send a message to the Oilers' coach: "I will not let you off easy, and you should have had your team better prepared."

After the game, Glanville did not shake Wyche's hand. Instead, he stomped to the locker room and blathered a few choice words about the Bengals' coach to the media.

There is a difference in sportsmanship and winning a game. But in the fight for your soul, the devil does not play fair either. This is why Christians need to run up the score and send the message to the enemy that he does not have a chance. Be prepared to win at all costs.

Do you want to send a message to the devil to tell him he has no chance to win in the fight for your life?

> *No, in all these things we are more than conquerors through him who loved us.*
>
> —Romans 8:37

Huddle Up

Satan is real and is out to win. He wants your soul, and he wants to destroy you. But it's your job to be strong and be ready.

Quick Snap

Here are some actions to take to stand firm and ensure victory:

1. Make a point to read the Bible through in a year. Once you finish, start again. When you find a play that works, continue to run it to perfection.
2. Find and become involved in a regular Bible study once a week or perhaps monthly. The key is to be consistent and participate. If you cannot find one, start one. Begin with some friends, and discover how stronger you can become in the Word of God.
3. Form an accountability group. This can be a group of friends who meet on a regular basis to talk about their successes and failures. Ask each member to hold you accountable for your actions, and do the same for them. When there is someone to answer to, you grow stronger and are less prone to mess up. "As iron sharpens iron, so one person sharpens another" (Proverbs 27:17).
4. Start and keep a daily journal. This does not have to be lengthy, but it may include what events took place throughout the day. You can include both prayers and fears. Go back and read them again on occasion to find out where you are on your journey.
5. Make a chart of prayer requests. You will find great delight when you are able to check off an answered prayer.

When you take part in activities to make you stronger in the Lord, you discover a way to blow out the forces of evil and pour it on the enemy. Who Dey!

Week 5

LEAVE NO DOUBT OF YOUR WITNESS

They all wept as they embraced him and kissed him. What grieved them most was his statement that they would never see his face again. Then they accompanied him to the ship.
—Acts 20:37–38

Boomer Esiason went out the way he planned. For his first nine years he wore the stripes; he was the heart and soul of the offense. He earned MVP honors and Pro-Bowl selections while he posted a record of 62-61 and threw for 27,149 yards with 187 TD for an overall rating of 83.1.

After three years in New York and one in Arizona, he found himself back in the Queen City for one last hurrah.

As a backup to Jeff Blake, he accepted his role. But toward the last half of a dismal year, he was thrust into the lineup to finish out the season. In the final five games, he went 4-1 as a starter and fired thirteen touchdown passes for a 106.9 rating.

The flashy signal caller went out with a "boom."

On the final throw of his career, Esiason fired a 77-yard TD pass to Darnay Scott against Baltimore on December 21, 1997, and the Bengals won the game 16-14.

Cincinnati fans loved his gunslinger style and leadership and will always remember his final play. He left a remarkable impression for the black and orange.

What will people say about you when you depart this life? Were you a Christian? Is there any doubt you served the Lord to the fullest? Could your loved ones recall your testimony, or would another memory come to mind?

Finally, brothers and sisters, rejoice! Strive for full restoration, encourage one another, be of one mind, live in peace. And the God of love and peace will be with you.

—2 Corinthians 13:11

Huddle Up

There are times when we choose work over other activities in our lives. The problem comes when we do this too often. Do you find you're at the office too much? Providing for your household is admirable, but when this consumes your time and energy, it may become an issue. When you spend too much time at work, you tend to neglect your family. You have to ask yourself, "Is it worth it to miss my child's game or school play?" "Is it worth it for my spouse to eat alone at the dinner table?"

Quick Snap

In today's busy environment and society, a person can lose focus on what his priorities need to be. Avoid the distractions Satan uses to trap you, and do your best to concentrate on what means the most:

1. God. He is the reason we exist and have our possessions. "But seek first his kingdom and his righteousness, and all these things will be given to you as well" (Matthew 6:33).
2. Family. Your loved ones are gifts from the Lord. Take care of your children, parents, brothers, sisters, or special friends. Love them and spend time with them when you can. "Anyone who does not provide for their relatives, and especially for their own household, has denied the faith and is worse than an unbeliever" (1 Timothy 5:8).
3. Church. You should take your family to church on a regular basis, not just when you feel like going. Establish yourself in a solid, fundamental, and Bible-believing church. "To him be glory in the church and in Christ Jesus throughout all generations, for ever and ever! Amen" (Ephesians 3:21).
4. Country. Teach your children to honor and respect the heritage of our nation. You have great freedoms because you are allowed by God to live here. Always be thankful for your country. "The Lord is a warrior; the Lord is his name" (Exodus 15:3).
5. Work. Take pride in your occupation and be faithful and dedicated. But keep in mind why you have a job, and don't lose sight of your obligations. Your family depends on you to provide an income, but they also rely on you to be present to lead them. You can juggle the routine of life. Your job is important, and there will be times you have to work overtime. But do it because you have to and not because you want to.

> "For I saw that there is nothing better for a person than to enjoy their work, because that is their lot. For who can bring them to see what will happen after them?" (Ecclesiastes 3:22).

When your priorities align with God's plan, you are remembered and respected by your friends and family. At the end of your life, your fans can recall the long touchdown that won the game. Who Dey!

Week 6

BE DEDICATED TO YOUR TEAM

Let love and faithfulness never leave you; bind them around your neck, write them on the tablet of your heart.
—Proverbs 3:3

Cincinnati Bengals quarterback Andy Dalton has his priorities in order. He practices long hours at his craft, dedicates time in the community to give back, helps those around him improve, and lets the whole world know he's married—even when he's on the football field.

For a few understandable reasons, many football players do not wear a wedding band when they play. There is a risk of injury if the jewelry gets caught on a jersey. A player might break his finger, or he may lose the valuable token on the field.

Coincidentally, a man who attended Dalton's own alma mater, Texas Christian University, developed a rubber ring for active athletes to wear. For Dalton, it was a perfect fit.

The All-Pro signal caller likes the concept so much he wears the bands everywhere he goes—even into the huddle.

"I am married, and to wear a ring and not have to worry about it getting damaged is nice," he said. "I want everyone to know I'm married, and I have no reason to take this ring off."

Dalton even color coordinates his bands with his uniforms. When the team is on the road and wears white jerseys, he puts on the white ring. At home, the black one makes an appearance. He wants to show Cincinnati, his colleagues, and the world he is off the market, even when he's on the field.

Do those around you know you are committed? Do you wear your ring if you can? Are you dedicated to your spouse? Christ showed His loyalty to His children when He laid down His life. The rings He wears are on the constant scars in the palms of His hands where the nails pieced His flesh.

He who finds a wife finds what is good and receives favor from the Lord.

—Proverbs 18:22

Huddle Up

Wearing a wedding ring to demonstrate your love for your wife is great, but anyone can do that whether their marriage is fantastic or on the rocks. Back up the symbolism by giving your wife true love, loyalty, respect, and devotion every day. Show her she is the most important person in the world to you by spending time with her and focusing on her needs. Satan is hard at work with temptations and distractions he uses to destroy your marriage and family, and you must take your wife's hand in prayer and stand strong together to fight for God's blessings on your home and your future together.

Quick Snap

You know what call to make. In your heart, there is no question. There are no excuses. Be true to your spouse no matter the circumstance. If there has been a trust issue, step up in the pocket and deliver a pass to the right receiver. Be a man with integrity. Stay focused on the task at hand and stick to your game plan. Victory is just in sight. Here are some suggestions on how to show your dedication to your spouse:

1. Show her love. Do your best to nurture and cherish your wife. There might be circumstances outside of your control, but always show love. Protect her from harm, be tender, and try to understand her needs.
2. Show her respect. This always needs to be the case, but even more so if there are children involved. Little ears and eyes hear and see what goes on in the home. A man of faith must always demonstrate and show honor and respect to his wife. Never berate her or make her feel less of a person. Pray with her and attend church together. Work as a team and hold each other accountable.
3. Show her leadership. As the man of the home, you are to lead by example. This does not give you authority to be a dictator. Pray and ask for God's guidance. Share decisions with your spouse, be flexible yet stern. Take everyone's circumstances into consideration before a conclusion is reached.
4. Show her attention. Little acts you think are insignificant to you might be major to her. A simple call or

two throughout the day or a surprise gift at the office will let her know you care. Help around the house with dishes, or wash the clothes yourself one day. Let her know you are still and always attracted to her.
5. Show her devotion. This is true in all situations—good times and bad. There might be emotional, physical, or financial issues to deal with in life. Christ loved the church and you so much He sacrificed His life for mankind. Honor your spouse and let her know you are ready to do whatever it takes to defend her. Stay faithful and true. Wear your ring and take pride in your marriage. "A wife of noble character who can find? She is worth far more than rubies" (Proverbs 31:10)

When you take a stand and let everyone know you are married and proud to be with your partner for life, doubt and insecurity will flee. Dalton steps up and delivers in the clutch while thousands of people watch. His fans not only see the football sail through the air and into the grasp of a receiver for a score, but they also see a sign of commitment on his finger and know he's a man who is dedicated to his marriage. Who Dey!

Week 7

DON'T WASTE TIME

Show me, Lord, my life's end and the number of my days; let me know how fleeting my life is. You have made my days a mere handbreadth; the span of my years is as nothing before you. Everyone is but a breath, even those who seem secure.
—Psalm 39:4–5

Cincinnati won its first-ever post-season game on January 3, 1982, against Buffalo 28-21. The Bengals, the AFC Champs, had not posted a playoff win in their previous three attempts.

Quarterback Ken Anderson found wide receiver Chris Collinsworth with 10:40 to play in the game for a sixteen-yard touchdown. The score boosted the Cincinnati lead to 28-21.

Buffalo, the AFC Wild Card team, mounted a comeback to tie the game and moved the ball to the Cincinnati red zone with about three minutes to play.

The Who-Dey defense stiffened and forced a fourth down. But the Bills could not get a play off in regulation and were called for a delay of game. The penalty hampered the efforts of the offense and turned the ball back over to Cincinnati. The delay-of-game flag cost them any chance to send the game into overtime to try for the win.

Do you waste time? Do you know your limits? Is your focus on temporal preoccupations or godly works? Can you do more with the moments God has given you?

Be very careful, then, how you live—not as unwise but as wise, making the most of every opportunity, because the days are evil. Therefore, do not be foolish, but understand what the Lord's will is.

—Ephesians 5:15–17

Huddle Up

You must realize at some point our life span is a gift from God, and we will never get it back. In today's society, video games and electronic devices have taken over the world. While there is nothing wrong with these hobbies, they become a problem when you allow them to consume you. Is your routine to watch television or play video games in your downtime? Admit you are in a rut, and get involved in more significant activities.

Quick Snap

Here are some suggestions to keep yourself focused on what is important in God's eyes:

1. Make the Lord your priority. You can still take part in pastimes you enjoy, such as video games or work on your car. But recognize you also have work to perform for the kingdom. In Hebrews, you are told to

throw away activities that hinder. Run with perseverance the race marked for you. Ask yourself if there is a sick person in the hospital you can visit instead of flipping on a video game.

2. Establish discipline in your walk with Christ. Just like you set aside time to "waste," you should plan to spend time with God. Establish a scheduled period when you volunteer for a charity or help out at a food shelter. Proverbs tells you whoever heeds discipline shows the way of life. Strike a healthy balance between time allowed for pleasure and time filled with God.

3. Never procrastinate. This can develop into a bad habit. Good intentions will not become reality without action. Make a list of the goals you want to achieve over the next few months to honor the Lord and start the wheels in motion. You might join a Bible study group or learn to play an instrument. Ecclesiastes 11:4 says whoever keeps staring at the wind won't sow; whoever daydreams won't reap. Get started on your task today.

4. Maintain a solid work ethic. No matter what you do for God, make sure you show enthusiasm and diligence. Never seek personal glory, and make sure you lift up others and the Lord. If you want to start a ministry, seek God's approval first, then give it your all once you receive His confirmation. You might stumble along the way, but keep your focus on His big plan.

Downtime and rest is normal and necessary to recharge, but don't become a lazy sloth. Get out and work for the kingdom.

> *Do everything in love.*
> —1 Corinthians 16:14

Don't delay your game but burst forward across the goal line with a firm purpose. Who Dey!

Week 8

MAKE THE MOST OF YOUR SECOND CHANCE

Yet this I call to mind and therefore I have hope: Because of the Lord's great love we are not consumed, for his compassions never fail. They are new every morning; great is your faithfulness.

—Lamentations 3:21–23

The season opener for the Bengals in 1981 did not go as planned for quarterback Ken Anderson. The team trailed 21-0 to visiting Seattle, and his stats were dismal.

Anderson had completed five of fifteen attempts for thirty-nine yards. Coach Forrest Gregg pulled the popular QB and gave Turk Schonert an opportunity. Cincinnati came back, and the stand-in rallied the team to a 27-21 victory.

A couple days after the victory, Anderson, a fan favorite in the Queen City, convinced Gregg to give him another shot to start against the New York Jets. The two met and Anderson made his case why he should be put under center. Gregg finally agreed and the Bengals won 31-30. Anderson went on to have the best year of his career. He threw for 3,754 yards with twenty-nine TDs and a passer rating of 98.4. He was named the league MVP and Offensive Player of the Year and led the Bengals to their first Super Bowl appearance.

Gregg could have stuck with backup Schonert, but he showed compassion and gave the veteran player Anderson another opportunity to redeem himself.

Have you asked for and received a second chance? How did you use it to accomplish something good? How did you turn the corner and come back better than ever?

If we confess our sins, he is faithful and just and will forgive us our sins and purify us from all unrighteousness.

—1 John 1:9

Huddle Up

Perhaps you have not performed well, either on the job or at home. Perhaps you have fumbled some opportunities in life and find yourself on the bench. What adjustments are you ready to make? Are you content to sit back and watch someone else take over your position, or will you fight to get your life back?

Quick Snap

To get a second chance from God, your spouse or your child, follow these suggestions. These steps might not be easy, but there is a price to pay for the thrill of victory:

1. Repent. You must admit you made a mistake in order to ask for forgiveness. Do not blame anyone else. Take full responsibility, and own your mishaps. "For the Lord your God is gracious and compassionate. He will not turn his face from you if you return to him" (2 Chronicles 30:9).
2. Recognize your problem. If you are a substance abuser, get away from the source. If the failure is moral, remove the temptation. No matter what causes you to slip, take a firm stance and toss a flag on the opponents. Better yet, kick them out of the game.
3. Restitution is key. When you make wrongs right, you put yourself in a position to win the game of life. This may be difficult, but you must put aside pride and exhibit humility.
4. Promise to do better. Seek God's help in this step. Look for Bible studies or other ways to demonstrate your genuine sincerity. Everyone makes mistakes and has a bad game. But you must recognize your faults and rise above the situation.
5. Start anew. This can excite you and scare you at the same time. You know you have been forgiven, so that's the cool part. The frightening part is to begin fresh. You might be married for twenty-six years and

have to start over to earn your spouse's trust—and that can take time. Look at the big picture, and be dedicated enough to see it through. You might have to face your addiction one day at a time. But each day of victory draws you closer to the Lord and shows others God's saving grace.

When you plead to God for another chance, He will give it to you. Keep in mind He is not a "genie in a bottle" who exists to get you out of trouble. God loves and cares about His children and wants the best for you. Take full advantage of the do-over. Ken Anderson did and had a banner year. You can too. Ask Jesus, your family, or friends for the opportunity. Accept their forgiveness, and go on to become the Most Valuable Person you can be. Who Dey!

Week 9

COME THROUGH IN THE CLUTCH

Whoever can be trusted with very little can also be trusted with much, and whosoever is dishonest with very little will also be dishonest with much.

—Luke 16:10

Bengals kicker Jim Breech made up for his miss in big fashion. He muffed a forty-yard attempt in the first quarter and retreated to the sideline under a barrage of boos from the Cincinnati home crowd.

But he had a chance in overtime to secure a win and much more. He could save his team's perfect home win season, the AFC Title, and a bye in the first round of the playoffs. No pressure, right?

Breech didn't succumb to the pressure as he drilled a twenty yarder with 7:01 left to play in OT to give the Bengals a 20-17 win. He might have been the smallest member of the team, but he delivered in a mighty big way.

Does this describe you? Do you live as Jesus did? Will you come through when needed by your friends or family? Can the

Master count on you when the going gets tough to proclaim your faith in Christ?

> *But if anyone obeys his word, love for God is truly made complete in them. This is how we know we are in him. Whoever claims to live in him must live as Jesus did.*
>
> —1 John 2:5–6

Huddle Up

You can always count on Christ, but what if the tables were turned? What if you could not depend on Christ? Whom would you pray to? Who would hear your cries? The truth is, God is dependable. He is able. He is always true. Are you? Do your loved ones trust and depend on you? Do you come through in the clutch when needed? If not, it isn't too late.

Quick Snap

Here are some characteristics for you to model that can make you the go-to-guy in your circle:

1. Be available: "I have no one else like him, who will show genuine concern for your welfare" (Philippians 2:20).

    Put your own needs last and your family's first. This means if you want to work late to get the overtime and your child has a school play—go watch the performance.

2. Be bold: "Now, Lord, consider their threats and enable your servants to speak your word with great boldness" (Acts 4:29).

   Speak up in a time of indecision or doubt. If your faith is under question, defend your beliefs with boldness. Never let anyone ridicule your Lord or your convictions.

3. Be compassionate: "Rejoice with those who rejoice; mourn with those who mourn" (Romans 12:15).

   When you take time to let others know you share in their emotion and can relate to their sorrow, your character is molded in a positive way.

4. Be determined: "Being strengthened with all power according to his glorious might so that you may have great endurance and patience" (Colossians 1:11).

   Don't let anything deter your service to the Lord or his house. Go to church on a regular basis with your family. Show them you are a dedicated follower of Christ. You might be placed in a situation to deliver a win in overtime. Make sure you are lined up properly and read the Word of God. Keep your head down and pray every day. Be ready when the time is right and step up to deliver the kick through the uprights.

5. Be forgiving: "Get rid of all bitterness, rage and anger, brawling and slander, along with every form of malice. Be kind and compassionate to one another, forgiving each other, just as in Christ God forgave you" (Ephesians 4:31–32).

   Mercy needs to be a major part of your life. People are going to hurt and disappoint you. Always forgive

but protect yourself and your family's reputation and interests. Forgiving someone doesn't mean you have to be become buddies. Show love, but don't let others take advantage of you on a regular basis.
6. Be grateful: "Give thanks to the Lord, for he is good; his love endures forever" (1 Chronicles 16:34).
Lose all traits of arrogance and be humble and thankful. Without God's grace, you have nothing. When you acknowledge this and demonstrate a heart of gratitude, you can grow in your walk with the Lord.

These are a few of the attributes to try to emulate each day. In your journey with God, you want to be the one He calls on in the clutch. He might want you to visit someone, go on a mission trip, or lead a Bible study. Come through when He puts you in a game-winning situation. Who Dey!

Week 10

YOU TOO CAN MAKE A COMEBACK

I will save you from the hands of the wicked and deliver you from the grasp of the cruel.

—Jeremiah 15:21

The Bengals trailed 20-3 at the start of the fourth quarter. The offense sputtered, and most people thought Baltimore had the game in the bag.

But quarterback Carson Palmer had other plans. He orchestrated a twenty-four-point, fourth-quarter comeback that caught the eyes of the NFL world. Not only did Cincinnati win 27-26, but they made it known they were a team to be reckoned with in the AFC.

Palmer was spectacular in the final stanza as he threw for two hundred yards and completed ten of eleven passes for three touchdowns. The win was a comeback for the ages.

Have you ever felt you had no chance to win or felt that the enemy had the win in the bag? Have you backslidden, and the road back to the Lord looks too hard to walk? Can you make a comeback?

I sought the Lord, and he answered me; he delivered me from all my fears. Those who look to him are radiant; their faces are never covered with shame.

—Psalm 34:4–5

Huddle Up

There may be times when you've drifted in your prayer life and don't read your Bible on a regular basis. Or maybe your church attendance has faltered too. It could be that you have grown cold in your Christian journey. It's not that you are a bad person, but you find you neglect God more and more. Enough is enough—make the comeback.

Quick Snap

You have decided you must return to the Lord in order to be happy again. What can you do? How do you revive your faith? First and foremost, you must ask God to forgive you and come back into your life. Once you have taken this critical step, there are other goals you can work toward to stay strong in the faith. The actions below will help you to get back into the game:

1. Make prayer a priority. Maintain a daily prayer schedule, and set aside a regular time to spend in conversation with your heavenly Father. Don't always present a laundry list of your wants, but rather spend much of the time in praise to God. Tell Him how grateful you are for another chance, and thank Him

for the gracious sacrifice He made for you. "Let us come before him with thanksgiving and extol him with music and song" (Psalm 95:2).

2. Get back in church. You can't win a game unless you are on the field. The same philosophy applies to your Christian journey. You must be around your teammates in order to be successful. Attend services on a regular basis even when you hear that voice tell you to stay home. Fellowship with other Christians feeds your spirit and connects you to a wonderful support system. "For where two or three are gathered in my name, there am I among them" (Matthew 18:20 ESV).

3. Become involved in church activities. Find your niche and get active. If you like to drive, offer to pick up people in the church van. If you have a talent to sing, ask the choir director how to join. If you enjoy teaching, find out how to become a Sunday School teacher. When you become active, you have a sense of fulfillment and want to serve the Lord even more. "Will you not revive us again, that your people may rejoice in you?" (Psalm 85:6).

4. Join or lead a Bible study. Talk to your pastor about available Bible study groups. If you cannot find one, consider and pray about launching one yourself. This might occur each week or month, but the point is to find a Biblical activity that brings you closer to the Lord. "Do your best to present yourself to God as one approved, a worker who does not need to be ashamed and who correctly handles the word of truth" (2 Timothy 2:15).

5. Read your Bible each day. Set a goal to read God's Word through in a year. Once you are finished, begin again from the top or follow a study guide. An accomplished NFL player knows the playbook. The same applies for a Believer. Dive into the Word of God, and become familiar with the Lord's instructions. Read it all, cover to cover. "For the word of God is alive and active. Sharper than any double-edged sword, it penetrates even to dividing soul and spirit, joints and marrow; it judges the thoughts and attitudes of the heart" (Hebrews 4:12).

If you think you are the only person who has grown cold and drifted away from the presence of the Lord, know you are not alone. The key is to make the comeback and win the game in the end. You can do it—you just have to want to be victorious. Who Dey!

Week 11

BECOME INDUCTED INTO GOD'S HALL OF FAME

But citizenship is in heaven. And we eagerly await a Savior from there, the Lord Jesus Christ.
—Philippians 3:20

The day is one every player in the NFL dreams about, but few ever see it come true.

Anthony Muñoz's first love was baseball. He dreamed of being a success on the diamond, but the gridiron had better plans for him. His NFL career culminated when the Pro Football Hall of Fame enshrined the beloved Bengal on August 1, 1998. He became the first player from Cincinnati to be inducted in Canton, Ohio.

A beautiful bronze statue tells all who visit the Hall that he was one of the greatest players in the NFL. He is also among the select few who were inducted on the first ballot.

His achievements on the field are remarkable. He started 182 games out of 185, was selected to play in eleven Pro Bowls, drew nine First Team All Pro honors, won Man of the Year in

1991, and was one of three unanimous selections to the NFL's All-Decade Team of the 1980s.

He is regarded by many to be the best offensive lineman to play the game. But when you talk with Muñoz, he will tell you this is not how he wants to be remembered. His main priority is his Lord and Savior Jesus Christ. He wants people to first think of him as a Christian, a husband, a father, and then a football player.

He is forever enshrined in Canton, but he longs for the day when he makes heaven his home—his ultimate trophy.

Set your minds on things above, not earthly things.
—Colossians 3:2

Huddle Up

What have you accomplished that would put you in God's hall of fame? Are you on a path to reach heaven? Is your life's main goal to reach the place God has prepared for you?

Quick Snap

Maybe you think you live a good life. But is it good enough? Here are some ways you can assure your entrance into God's promised land:

1. Repent and be saved. This is the only way to make it to glory. Confess your sins to Jesus, and ask Him to come live in your heart. Now you are ready to do some good. "Repent, then, and turn to God, so that your sins may be wiped out, that times of refreshing may come from the Lord" (Acts 3:19).

2. Help others. You must put your needs last. God will take care of you. But when you help those in despair, Christ takes note. "For I was hungry and you gave me something to eat, I was thirsty and you gave me something to drink, I was a stranger and you invited me in" (Matthew 25:35).
3. Treat others with respect. Never judge your neighbor. Set the example and be the light to those around you. "So, in everything, do to others what you would have them do to you" (Matthew 7:12).
4. Read the Word of God. We can't hear God's voice if we don't spend time with Him. Establish a comfortable pace to read the Scripture through in a year. This might take about twenty minutes or more per day and will draw you closer to the Lord. Be dedicated and set aside time to spend in the Bible. This might mean you get up thirty minutes earlier each day or sacrifice some of your lunch time.
5. Pray. Talk to your heavenly Father often. Cast your burdens on Him, and He will deliver you in times of trouble.
6. Be thankful. When you demonstrate a grateful heart and humility, you appreciate the blessings the Lord has given you.
7. Forgive. Where are you without God's mercy? Remember He did this for you, and you must show the same mercy to others. "For if you forgive other people when they sin against you, your heavenly Father will also forgive you" (Matthew 6:14).

    This does not mean to let people take you for granted but exercise grace and boldness at the same time.

8. Testify. As a disciple of Christ, you are to witness to others about His saving grace. This can be done in subtle ways. You don't have to be a preacher to get the word out. Do it in your own special and unique way. Let the light of Christ shine through you.
9. Attend church. Muñoz would not have been a successful player if he had not practiced and played the game. You must be present to be effective and learn about Him.
10. Praise. The devil doesn't want us to worship the Lord. Have regular talks with Christ, not just in the times of struggle. You don't have to be in church to honor the King. Praise Him and thank Him often throughout each day.

Heaven is the ultimate reward for the Christian who is dedicated to live a holy life in the eyes of God. Anthony Muñoz did right in the opinions of his peers and found everlasting fame in the eyes of the NFL world. Where will you spend your life after your time on earth? Who Dey!

Week 12

PLAY LIKE A CHAMPION

So, David triumphed over the Philistine with a sling and a stone; without a sword in his hand he struck down the Philistine and killed him.

—1 Samuel 17:50

Boomer Esiason returned to the Cincinnati Bengals in a backup role after three years in New York and one in Arizona. He was thirty-six years old and in the twilight of his career.

Jeff Blake started at QB but experienced issues under the helm, so Cincinnati Coach Bruce Coslet thought some veteran experience might be what his squad needed. Esiason, a former league MVP, was tapped to finish the last five games of the season.

Esiason had just come off the bench the previous week to rescue the team from defeat, and now he was back in familiar territory—under center on the first team.

On November 22, 1997, he led the Bengals to a 31-26 win over visiting Jacksonville. He looked better than ever. The fast-paced, no-huddle offense was in fifth gear and poured it on the Jaguar defense. He tossed two first-half TD passes and orchestrated a 97-yard drive toward the end of the half to post a 28-10 lead.

The left-handed gunslinger overcame his obstacle of time and slew any myths he was finished as a professional quarterback.

How do you fight your enemy? Do you have what it takes to play like a champion?

> *David ran and stood over him. He took hold of the Philistine's sword and drew it from the sheath. After he killed him, he cut off his head with the sword. When the Philistines saw that their hero was dead, they turned and ran.*
>
> —1 Samuel 17:51

Huddle Up

No matter where you are in your Christian walk, the devil wants to defeat you. You might be a Christian rookie or a veteran. Nonetheless, you are a target. Are you prepared to play to win? Do you practice every day for the moment when the coach puts you into the game? Be ready to fight and conquer.

Quick Snap

Here are some characteristics of a true champion on the Lord's team:

1. Expect to triumph. In fact, read the book of Revelation because it declares Christ and His church the winners of the game. It is a wonderful feeling to know the battle has already been won. All you

have to do is show up and play. Another good verse to support victory is: "But thanks be to God! He gives us the victory through our Lord Jesus Christ" (1 Corinthians 15:57).

2. Never make an excuse when you lose. Instead, focus on what you can do better as a believer for the next game. Become stronger and wiser through mistakes. Grow, learn, and be determined not to make the same missteps again. Own them, repent, and put them in the past. "For though the righteous fall seven times, they rise again" (Proverbs 24:16).

3. Be confident in your beliefs. Your assurance grows when you read your Bible, attend church on a regular basis, pray, and tell others about God's love and mercy. Always be prepared to be called off the bench. You don't have to make the headlines, just be ready to do your part. Esiason was a backup when Coslet looked to him to revive the team. Accept your role and play like a champ. "I can do all things through Him who strengthens me" (Philippians 4:13 ESV).

4. Focus on what you get to do and not on what you have to do. Adopt a mindset where you never see your Christian responsibilities as a chore. You have been saved by the blood of Jesus Christ and are redeemed! Be thankful for every minute you have on earth. Esiason enjoyed his MVP glory days, but he now found himself regulated to the second team. However, he still loved to play the game. There may be unpleasant circumstances in life, but know you are on the victorious team. You get to go to church, you

get to pray, and you get to witness. Once you have this positive attitude, you can lead your team to a fourth-quarter comeback.
5. Celebrate all victories, not just the big one. Examine what the Lord has done for you. He gives you life every day. He gives you a place to sleep and puts bread on your table. Your family and job are blessings from Him. Don't get caught up in the one big prayer you want to be answered. When you celebrate the little victories, you are prepared for the big one to come.

When you have the attitude of a winner, you are better prepared to face the big battles in life. You may never face a true giant in the physical sense, but you may fight an enormous struggle. Be ready to come off the bench to take the championship. Who Dey!

Week 13

CELEBRATE YOUR SAVIOR

A time to weep and a time to laugh, a time to mourn and a time to dance.

—Ecclesiastes 3:4

Running back Ickey Woods is an icon in Cincinnati still today. The larger-than-life fullback played four years with the Bengals and is a fan favorite. He produced on the field and had a positive impact on the team. In thirty-seven games, he rushed for 1,525 on 332 carries. He averaged 4.6 yards per carry and romped into the end zone twenty-seven times. He was also selected to the All-Pro team in 1988.

Cincinnati reigned as AFC Champions in 1988, and Woods led the team with 1,066 yards on the ground and fifteen TDs. But he will most be remembered for his end-zone celebration dubbed "The Ickey Shuffle."

The description of the dance is well documented. He scored a touchdown against Cleveland at Riverfront Stadium in Cincinnati, and his celebration was a bit mundane. Rickey Dixon, the team's safety, told him he needed to get more creative and jazz it up some. He pondered and practiced, and a phenomenon was born.

Before a game against the New York Jets, he showed his new celebration to Dixon and received his approval. The dance took on a life bigger than the team. Everyone around the nation did the "Ickey Shuffle." Within weeks, it spread and took on even more notoriety when the Bengals reached the Super Bowl.

How do you praise the Lord? Do you lift your hands or dance? What benefit does a Christian receive from demonstrating glory to the Savior?

Let them praise his name with dancing and make music to him with timbrel and harp.

—Psalm 149:3

Huddle Up

Hopefully, deep down, you want to show praise and thanks for what God has done for you. But maybe you feel silly or a bit intimidated at the same time. You might frequent a church where the worshipers shout and run the aisles, or you may attend one that frowns on such demonstrations. The bottom line is you feel you don't give Him enough praise. So how do you change this?

Quick Snap

Here are some ideal ways to praise the Lord in church or anywhere your heart tells you. But if you do the "Ickey Shuffle" in a church service, don't spike the offering plate at the end:

1. Praise Him and lift your hands or arms toward heaven. This brings you closer to the Lord, and He desires your gratitude. "Lift up your hands in the sanctuary and praise the Lord" (Psalm 134:2).
2. Praise Him with words. A solid and thankful testimony is a wonderful way to give thanks to the Lord. Do not turn your story into a soap opera, and make sure your words honor and glorify the Lord. No one wants to hear about your problems, but they do want to hear how God comforted or rescued you in a terrible time. Be short and to the point, and give God all the credit. "So we say with confidence, 'The Lord is my helper, I will not be afraid, what can mere mortals do to me'" (Hebrews 13:6).
3. Praise Him in song. When a singer is anointed by God, this is a great way to glorify the Lord. If God has called you to this ministry, then do it for Him. "I will praise the Lord all my life; I will sing praise to my God as long as I live" (Psalm 146:2).
4. Praise Him in unison with others. When people are together and praise the Lord in the unity of the Holy Spirit, join in and become part of the movement. When you do this, you feel God's presence. "I will declare your name to my brothers and sisters; in the assembly I will sing your praises" (Hebrews 2:12).

5. Praise Him with instruments and dance. Be sure the dance is of the Lord and not something you practiced in your hallway. A dance to the Master is intimate and filled with the spirit. David danced before the Almighty with all of his might. This is something you should consider, however, clothing should be highly considered.

No matter how you praise the Lord, make sure your worship is genuine and not done for show. The end result is to give the Lord credit for all He has done for you. The "Ickey Shuffle" was a popular yet clumsy celebration every Bengals' fan loved. Celebrate God in style—your style. Who Dey!

Week 14

BE THE LEADER

Do nothing from selfishness or empty conceit, but with humility of mind regard one another as more important than yourselves.

—Philippians 2:3 NASB1995

For more than a decade, Tim Krumrie was the heart and soul of the Bengals' defense. He was feared and respected at the same time. In 188 games and twelve seasons, he missed four games. The defensive anchor of the Bengals finished his career with 1,008 tackles and 34.5 sacks, and he made two Pro Bowl appearances.

He is credited with giving Hall of Fame quarterback Brett Favre his chance to shine when he knocked out Green Bay Packers QB Don Majkowski in 1992. Favre took over the spot for good.

In 1988, Krumrie enjoyed the best year of his career. He led the team with 152 tackles and earned All-Pro honors. He took his team to Super Bowl XXIII where he shattered his leg early in the game. He is remembered for his refusal to leave the stadium to go to the hospital until after the game was over, despite two serious fractures.

He later coached in Cincinnati for seven years after he retired as a player. His name is associated with greatness and leadership.

Are you the leader? Are you willing to suffer through a little pain to watch the people under your care succeed? Will you sacrifice for your family?

He must increase, but I must decrease.
—John 3:30 ESV

Huddle Up

Your loved ones and children need your guidance. The last thing you want is for them to turn to someone else for direction. Your pastor is there for spiritual matters and for wisdom. But you need to rise to the occasion and be the one your household looks to for daily inspiration.

Quick Snap

Here are some ways you can establish leadership in your home. Remember, there is a difference between a leader and a dictator. You do not have to yell and scream to be an effective captain. The best leaders are servants. Follow these suggestions to better establish your role:

1. Pray with your spouse and children. Show them you care about their souls and their safety. Put them first.

"How good and pleasant it is when God's people live together in unity" (Psalm 133:1).

2. Show gratitude. Teach your family to demonstrate appreciation. "But thanks be to God! He gives us the victory through our Lord Jesus Christ" (1 Corinthians 15:57).
3. Do little acts, just because. Wash the dishes or do the laundry without being asked. Send your wife flowers for no reason. "Do everything in love" (1 Corinthians 16:14).
4. Establish spiritual goals for your loved ones. Read the Bible and attend church together on a regular basis. "Commit to the Lord whatever you do, and he will establish your plans" (Proverbs 16:3).
5. Take your spouse on a weekend getaway. Surprise her with an unannounced trip. Take care of all the details, and let her relax. "A wife of noble character who can find? She is worth far more than rubies" (Proverbs 31:10).
6. Take your kids on a weekend getaway. Get alone with them and talk about what you expect from them. Make the trip about them and teach them right from wrong. "Start children off on the way they should go, and even when they are old they will not turn from it" (Proverbs 22:6).
7. Teach your children discipline. This does not mean to rule with an iron fist, but be stern in love. "Fathers, do not exasperate your children; instead bring them up in the training and instruction of the Lord" (Ephesians 6:4).

8. Volunteer your time. Show how important it is to help others. "The father of a righteous child has great joy; a man who fathers a wise son rejoices in him" (Proverbs 23:24).
9. Worship with and in front of your family. "Let everything that has breath praise the Lord. Praise the Lord" (Psalm 150:6).
10. Admit mistakes. Don't be too proud to acknowledge when you are wrong. "You, Lord, are forgiving and good, abounding in love to all who call to you" (Psalm 86:5).

Your spouse and your children expect you to lead. Set a righteous example of holiness before them, and make it your life's goal for your entire family to serve the Lord before you leave this world. Who Dey!

Week 15

OVERCOME THE OBSTACLES

Do not be overcome by evil, but overcome evil with good.
—Romans 12:21

The tragic events of September 11, 2001, left the nation in shock. Life was far from normal, and people looked to the NFL for some temporary relief to take their minds off the horror for a few hours.

The Baltimore Ravens, fresh off a Super Bowl victory the season before, rolled into Paul Brown Stadium in Cincinnati favored to win.

Bengals quarterback Jon Kitna sent a message early in the game when he directed the opening drive that resulted in a touchdown throw to Corey Dillon. He followed up on the next series and scored himself on a draw from two yards out.

Cincinnati had control of the game from the start. Baltimore's twelve-game winning streak came to an end when linebacker Takeo Spikes intercepted an Elvis Grbac pass and returned the ball sixty-six yards for the score with six minutes to play in the game.

The Bengals forced six turnovers and overcame great odds to defeat the Ravens 21-10. The win was a complete team effort. The underdog did not back down and met the challenge head-on.

What obstacles have you overcome? Have you given the Lord the glory? Are you in a fight with the forces of evil?

> *But thanks be to God! He gives us the victory through our Lord Jesus Christ.*
> —1 Corinthians 15:57

Huddle Up

Battles are not enjoyable. At times, the enemy may have you pinned inside your own five-yard line. You might look up and see a defense ready to blitz and sack you for a safety. Your game plan for life has been stymied by an unannounced and unwelcome event. The easy way out is to give up and let the other team score. What play will you make?

Quick Snap

There is no victory without a fight. Oftentimes, difficult situations allow you to grow stronger as a believer. Break out of the huddle, approach the line, and be confident you can reach the first-down marker and get out of the hole. Consider these suggestions to help you battle back to victory:

1. Stop any behavior that might be even borderline sinful. You may have never before even considered this to be wrong. When you come to a crossroads,

examine your actions from the recent past. God might be sending you a message. "Therefore, since we are surrounded by such a great cloud of witnesses, let us throw off everything that hinders and the sin that so easily entangles. And let us run with perseverance the race marked out for us" (Hebrews 12:1).

2. Confront the doubt in your thoughts. Don't let the issue run a post route in your mind, but rather call a safety blitz and focus on the positive aspects in life. This does not mean to forget the obstacles you face, but realign the way you think. Put the Lord on the front line and let Him rush the quarterback. "Who is it that overcomes the world? Only the one who believes that Jesus is the Son of God" (1 John 5:5).

3. Submit yourself and trust in the Lord to deliver. Everyone goes through struggles at times. These might be financial, physical, emotional, or spiritual. The hardest thing to do, yet the best option, is to turn your worry over to Christ. Pray and seek His wisdom and guidance. The human reaction is to fix a challenge yourself. Many times, this backfires, and you find yourself in a worse predicament. Look to the Savior. He never lets you down. "When I am afraid, I put my trust in you" (Psalm 56:3).

4. Trust God can overcome. The same Lord who raised Lazarus from the dead can help you in your time of crisis. Believe and wait. Do what the Master tells you, but ultimately remain patient for His purpose and plan. He takes care of the matter in His time—the best time. "Trust in the Lord with all your heart and

lean not on your own understanding; in all your ways submit to him and he will make your paths straight" (Proverbs 3:5–6).
5. Learn from the experience. You might be placed into this scenario for a divine reason. Take into consideration He may use this to prepare you to help someone else who goes through a similar trial in the future. He wants you to praise Him in advance for the way He is able to deliver you. In all cases, give Him thanks. "He will not let your foot slip—he who watches over you will not slumber" (Psalm 121:3).

Life is full of battles and obstacles. Your reaction determines if you are an All-Pro. The natural and human response is to try to handle them yourself. Don't run from a negative circumstance, but meet it head-on with the Lord leading the charge. Who Dey!

Week 16

ENCOURAGE OTHERS

Therefore encourage one another and build each other up, just as in fact you are doing.

—1 Thessalonians 5:11

The Marvin Lewis era in Cincinnati came at the right time. It was 2003 and the franchise was in a downward spiral. The Bengals posted a mere nineteen wins over a five-year span. Morale had plunged to an all-time low and attendance evaporated.

Fans were cynical and pessimistic about any odds of a winning season. After the team announced Lewis as the new head coach, the fan base grew energized. He was the first defensive coordinator appointed by the Bengals to serve in this position and was well known for his orchestration of the Baltimore Ravens' defense that led them to a Super Bowl win in 2000.

His hire was a break from Cincinnati tradition. Owner Mike Brown had always selected a coach who had either played for or against his franchise. A new dawn had arisen.

Lewis's presence at the press conference brought instant excitement to the Queen City. Players and fans alike were now optimistic, hopeful, and encouraged again. It was similar to two thousand years ago when the world looked bleak until the savior, Jesus Christ, stepped in.

When you motivate those around you, great things can happen. A sense of hope often leads to wondrous results.

I have told you these things, so that in me you may have peace. In this world you will have trouble. But take heart! I have overcome the world.

—John 16:33

Huddle Up

When the time comes, will you be a source of inspiration or ignore the needs of your friend when he's depressed about a circumstance in his life? Will you encourage him when he says he doubts his salvation and wonders why God has not delivered him from the situation? Will you support him if he loses his job or experiences betrayal? Doing these things allows you to be Christ to him in these moments.

Quick Snap

Difficult situations are the perfect time for the ball to be snapped. Those times are perfect times to act because any delay could set your friend up for more disappointment. Take the ball and run right up the middle for the first down. Here are some plays to help you be an encouragement:

1. Pray with your friend in need: When you take time to reach out in prayer with a person who is down, it

shows you care. This is a special time you can share forever. When you place the needs of others before the throne of God, this lets them know they are not alone. "As iron sharpens iron, so one person sharpens another" (Proverbs 27:17).

2. Read scripture with him: This can help show comfort to your friend in need. What better way to inspire him than to share the Word of God? You can point him in the right direction with the Lord's help. "I will instruct you and teach you in the way you should go; I will counsel you with my loving eye on you" (Psalm 32:8).

3. Write a note: When you send a note or mail a letter to a person who is discouraged, it lifts his spirits. Your thoughtfulness can bring joy to a person when he receives an unexpected text with some uplifting words to help through a tough time. If you cannot be there in person, be there in the written word. Keep it brief and to the point. He will know you care. "Each of us should please our neighbors for their good, to build them up" (Romans 15:2).

4. Invite him to church: When you show support for a friend through his struggles, the Lord is pleased. When you worship the Lord together, you send a powerful message to your friend that he is not alone in the battle. "Praise the Lord, my soul; all my inmost being, praise his holy name" (Psalm 103:1).

5. Give him assurance: This is the most crucial part of encouragement. No matter what events take place, make sure your friend knows God is the Master of

the universe and takes care of His own. This does not mean He will bail someone out of a sticky situation. There are consequences for actions. But in the end, the Lord is all you need. "I lift up my eyes to the mountains—where does my help come from? My help comes from the Lord, the Maker of heaven and earth" (Psalm 121:1–2).

When Marvin Lewis was hired, a new day dawned in Cincinnati. There have since been struggles along with wonderful memories. But he provided a sense of hope at the time for those who had lost their zeal to root for the Bengals. You can be the spark plug to ignite those who are depressed. Be a Who Dey encourager. Who Dey!

Week 17

WHEN ADVERSITY HITS

But I tell you, love your enemies and pray for those who persecute you.

—Matthew 5:44

The play changed the outlook of the franchise forever.

January 8, 2006 was the AFC Wild Card playoff game against rival Pittsburgh. Cincinnati fans were confident this was their time. The Bengals were in their first playoff appearance in fourteen years, and quarterback Carson Palmer had experienced a terrific season. He boasted a 101.1 passer rating and threw for thirty-two touchdowns, the most in the league.

On the opening drive, he heaved a sixty-six-yard TD pass to Chris Henry. But while the crowd roared with jubilation, he lay on the ground in obvious pain. Former Bengal Kimo von Oelhoffen took out Palmer's knee along with any hope of a Super Bowl run. The QB was carted off the field with a shattered knee, and his team lost the game 31-17.

After surgery and a long recovery, he returned to the lineup the next season. He had another quality year as he threw for twenty-eight TDs and posted a passer rating of 93.9. He led the team to another playoff appearance in 2009, but they lost to the New York Jets in Cincinnati.

Palmer was knocked down, but he came back to play another day. The devil wants to take our feet out from under us. He'll do anything to put us out of the game. We need to decide if we're going to get back up to play again.

How do you react when trials come? Will you get back on your feet or let the devil take you out of the game?

Bless those who persecute you; bless and do not curse.
—Romans 12:14

Huddle Up

Tough times seem to come out of nowhere. Perhaps you have been sideswiped by an incident you did not see on the horizon. You may have lost your job or your relationship with a special person has gone sour. Maybe a loved one has been diagnosed with a terminal condition. No matter the circumstance, you are injured. Do you ever wonder where God is in these situations?

Quick Snap

You are not invincible, nor are you alone. Everyone goes through trials. Some handle them better than others. If you are tempted to blame the Lord, don't. Problems in life come to all, and you go through them for a reason. Consider these examples of why Christ allows you to go through difficult times:

1. A trial exposes your weaknesses. When you accept what has happened and embrace the situation, you can experience the mighty power of the Lord in your life. Trust in Him to use your circumstance to increase your faith. "But he said to me, 'My grace is sufficient for you, for my power is made perfect in weakness.' Therefore, I will boast all the more gladly about my weaknesses, so that Christ's power may rest on me. That is why, for Christ's sake, I delight in weaknesses, in insults, in hardships, in persecutions, in difficulties. For when I am weak, then I am strong" (2 Corinthians 12:9–10).
2. A trial brings you to your knees. The Lord hears your cries of humble repentance and covers you with His tender love and mercy. He wants you to draw close to him.
3. A trial gets your attention. Once you realize the issue is too big for you to handle, turn it over to the Master and trust His plan for your life.
4. A trial makes your dislike for sin become stronger. "Love must be sincere. Hate what is evil; cling to what is good" (Romans 12:9).
5. A trial removes pride. When you are hurt and vulnerable, all of your accomplishments are worthless. You must put vanity aside and ask God for help.
6. A trial reminds you the devil wants to destroy you. Satan strikes at any time. You must be on guard for the tricks he uses to attempt to wipe out your heart and soul. He does not announce his attacks, but you'll know when he hits. "Be alert and of sober mind. Your

enemy the devil prowls around like a roaring lion looking for someone to devour" (1 Peter 5:8).
7. A trial increases your faith. Step up your prayer life, and draw closer to God. Be sure when the storm is over, you continue to practice intense fellowship with the Savior. He is not a wish granter—He is your heavenly Father.
8. A trial forces you to examine your priorities and persuades you to put your life in perspective. You will begin to appreciate what is most important.
9. A trial reveals true friendship. A true friend sticks with you to the end. He supports you and even tells you what you don't want to hear. Casual acquaintances fade when the tough times come.
10. A trial directs your attention on God. He is the reason you are here and gives you what you need. Focus your eyes and heart on what He wants for you and your future.

No one chooses to go through trials and adversity. But when you are on the ground in pain, remember this is for a divine reason. God can help you to get through the situation and become even stronger. Never lose sight of the Lord, and ask Him to deliver you. Who Dey!

Week 18

WHAT DOES YOUR NAME SAY ABOUT YOU?

Do nothing out of selfish ambition or vain conceit. Rather, in humility value others above yourselves.
—Philippians 2:3

On October 27, 1967, Paul Brown announced the official name of the Cincinnati Bengals.

Other names considered included the Romans, the Krauts, and the Celtics. Some even speculated the team might be called the Buckeyes since Brown coached football at The Ohio State University from 1941 to 1943 and guided them to a national championship in 1942.

But a committee went with the name Bengals for a couple of reasons:

1. The name was previously used by a short-lived professional football team that played in Cincinnati from 1937 to 1941.
2. Animation potential for this mascot could attract families to the fan base.

This type of tiger also has a charismatic and royal feature, which attracted the owner to the name. He was fond of the persona of the animal because it combined fierceness and likeability at the same time.

When people hear your name, what comes to mind? Are you in good standing?

> *Your beauty should not come from outward adornment, such as elaborate hairstyle and the wearing of gold jewelry or fine clothes. Rather, it should be that of your inner self, the unfading beauty of a gentle and quiet spirit, which is of great worth in God's sight.*
>
> —1 Peter 3:3–4

Huddle Up

Your Christian reputation is important. You don't want people to think of you as a hypocrite or someone who does not live up to the standards of God's Word.

Quick Snap

Whether you are a babe in Christ or a longtime believer, here are some tips and practices to maintain a solid reputation and integrity. Some of these may sound basic, but they go a long way to help prevent someone from forming a negative opinion of you:

1. Practice what you preach. Once you establish a position on a topic, do not fold or waver.

2. Pay your bills. Do your best to live within your means. "The wicked borrow and do not repay, but the righteous give generously" (Psalm 37:21).
3. Keep your word. If you make a promise, then keep your commitment.
4. Tithe on a consistent basis. Remember, all blessings come from above. You may have put in long hours at work, but the Lord gave you the job and the income, and he commands 10 percent back. You cannot afford to stiff God. "Will a mere mortal rob God? Yet you rob me. But you ask, 'How are we robbing you?' In tithes and offerings" (Malachi 3:8).
5. Stay out of the gossip circle. This is a trap set by the devil. When he gets you to talk bad about other people, he's got you. "A gossip betrays a confidence, but a trustworthy person keeps a secret" (Proverbs 11:13).
6. Don't fall for the trick. Walk away. Put in an honest day of work. Show honor to your employer. Be true and honest. You might be the only Bible your employers and coworkers ever read.
7. Hold your tongue in check. Avoid these: "Haughty eyes, a lying tongue, hands that shed innocent blood" (Proverbs 6:17).
8. Volunteer your time. You may pitch in at a local homeless shelter, with a pro-life organization, or your home church. Set aside time each month to give back. Set an example to your family and community. "Love never fails. But where there are prophecies, they will cease; where there are tongues, they will be stilled; where there is knowledge, it will pass away" (1 Corinthians 13:8).

9. Pray. Talk to your heavenly Father each day to deepen your relationship with Christ.
10. Attend church. Take your loved ones to worship on a regular basis. Do not let events of the world keep you from the house of God.

When you practice these steps, your reputation will become stronger. In the long run, a good name helps you in business affairs, in a job hunt, or just day by day. You are called to be a faithful steward. Who Dey!

Week 19

WHERE IS YOUR COURAGE?

Have I not commanded you? Be strong and courageous. Do not be afraid; do not be discouraged, for the Lord your God will be with you wherever you go.

—Joshua 1:9

Fans of all ages pack out Paul Brown Stadium to cheer on the Bengals. The crowd comes to watch Andy Dalton connect with A. J. Green for a long touchdown pass, or they want to see a strong defensive stand.

But on November 6, 2014, all eyes at the stadium and around the nation were fixated on Leah Still, the four-year-old daughter of defensive tackle Devon Still. The little girl battled Stage 4 cancer (neuroblastoma). Her struggle caught the attention of the country, and she was honored at the game that day. Her father continued to play to draw awareness to her disease, even though his emotions ran rampant.

She had cancer all through her body, but she watched the game from Domata Peko's suite and waved to her father while he warmed up. The camera zoomed in on her, playing to the emotions of the crowd inside the stadium.

Cleveland Browns quarterback Brian Hoyer put the game aside at the end of the first quarter, crossed the line of scrimmage, and hugged Devon when the Bengals presented a $1.3 million check to Cincinnati Children's Hospital. Hoyer later said the youngster demonstrated true courage.

Today, Leah is fine. She is the face of the Leah Still Foundation and declares she has "beaten up cancer." A little girl showed big and strong football players how to stay tough in one of life's biggest battles.

Be on your guard; stand firm in the faith; be courageous; be strong.

—1 Corinthians 16:13

Huddle Up

Do you have courage? What does bravery mean to you? Have you ever found yourself in a difficult situation and were torn between right and wrong? One choice could cost you a job or a relationship. You know what to do—you just have to find the strength to make the best choice. Leah battled cancer with a smile and determination. How will you combat your foe?

Quick Snap

After you seek God's direction and guidance, you must now make the call. Once you do, this won't seem as hard as you thought and you may become emboldened. Taking a stand is similar to a ride on a roller coaster for the first time. The actual train and track intimidates and frightens you. But after you've ridden once, you want to do it again. Here are some ways to show courage in times of distress:

1. Say NO! Such a small word has a large impact. Maybe someone at work flirts with you or asks you to do something against your convictions. Use the word effectively and often if needed. When you establish boundaries, you score extra points with God and your spouse.
2. Break the chains. If you have people who toss up your past and flaunt it in your face, let them know you are forgiven and a new creature in God's eyes. Offer to share the gospel with them too. "Therefore, if anyone is in Christ, the new creation has come: The old has gone, the new is here" (2 Corinthians 5:17).
3. Stand for what is right. This might cost you some "friends" when your position is honorable but maybe not popular. Don't try to make people feel better with a wimpy stance. Stay strong. Just like in the movie *Braveheart*, William Wallace showed courage under fire and did not give in to the demands of the English monarch. Then there's the account of David vs. Goliath. Physically, David's chances were slim against the mighty warrior. But God showed favor due to his great courage and supplied him with what he needed to slay the enemy. David did not run from the fight. He let God lead the charge.

No matter what challenge you meet, always do what is right in the sight of the Lord. Choose courage over popularity, and you attract likeminded people to your team. Little Leah showed bold courage to men who were six feet nine inches tall and weighed 325 pounds. Size doesn't matter. Who Dey!

Week 20

PREPARE YOUR FAMILY

Fix these words of mine in your hearts and minds; tie them as symbols on your hands and bind them on your foreheads. Teach them to your children, talking about them when you sit at home and when you walk along the road, when you lie down and when you get up.

—Deuteronomy 11:18–19

Cincinnati Coach Forrest Gregg learned from one of the legends of the game. He played under Vince Lombardi in Green Bay in some bitter cold weather.

His mentor once practiced his team indoors to prepare for an NFL championship game against Philadelphia in 1960. The Packers lost the game 17-13, and Lombardi never took his team inside to play again.

Gregg was part of five NFL titles with the final one coming in minus-thirteen-degree temperatures. The Ice Bowl of 1967 brought back memories for the coach when his Bengals played in minus nine degrees (with a windchill factor of minus fifty-nine) on January 10, 1982. A win would give Cincinnati its first ever Super Bowl appearance.

The weather was so cold that San Diego Chargers owner Gene Klein asked Bengals Assistant General Manager Mike Brown to postpone the game. Brown knew the winter chills might stifle the productive pass attack of the Chargers' quarterback Dan Fouts and said, "No!"

Meanwhile, Gregg held practice outside in frigid weather all week. In the end, the Bengals played magnificently and won the game 27-7 in what has been dubbed the "Freezer Bowl."

Have you prepared your family to follow Christ? Have you learned from the elders in the church to do what is right in the eyes of the Lord? Have you practiced for the fight?

> *Write them on the doorframes of your houses and on your gates, so that your days and the days of your children may be many in the land the Lord swore to give your ancestors, as many as the days that the heavens are above the earth.*
>
> —Deuteronomy 11:20–21

Huddle Up

Your home team will encounter many different temperatures in life. There are hot days and cold, and instances of success and failure, laughter and sadness. Are your team and loved ones ready to play, no matter what the conditions are?

Quick Snap

Here are some ways to make sure your family is prepared, especially on that day when the Lord returns to take his team to the greatest Super Bowl of all:

1. Pray together as a unit. Set aside time to do this on a regular basis.
2. Take turns and memorize scripture. Make time in the Word fun. Set prizes and rewards when your youngsters accomplish a goal.
3. Hold weekly devotions. Ask each of your children to lead a devotion once a month.
4. Make sure you dedicate time to spend with your spouse and your kids. Your job is important, but make your household a priority. Emails and text messages can wait.
5. Attend church together. This is crucial. If your child rebels, take them anyway. You are their parent—not their best friend.
6. Encourage your teens to hang out with Christian friends who share their same values.
7. Establish rules and boundaries. Enforce your laws and establish consequences for violations. Adolescents expect and desire guidance.
8. Make the day you attend church your family day. The TV has an off button for a reason.
9. Let your sons and daughters hear you pray for them. This can have a tremendous and positive impact on their lives.
10. Love your kids, and never place conditions on them.

When you take these steps, you have done your part to prepare your family for the frigid winds they may face in life. Forrest Gregg learned an early lesson the hard way and tasted bitter defeat, which prepared him for future victories. Do your part and set the example. Embrace the cold and have your team ready to play. Who Dey!

Week 21

A FRESH START

See, I am doing a new thing! Now it springs up; do you not perceive it? I am making a way in the wilderness and the streams in the wasteland.

—Isaiah 43:19

A fresh start can encourage a new perspective. Such was the case when Jeff Blake took over as the quarterback of the Cincinnati Bengals on October 30, 1994. He was the third string quarterback and got the nod when David Klinger and Don Hollas were both injured the previous week.

Cincinnati had lost twenty-six of the previous thirty games, and expectations hung low among the fan base. But the defending Cowboys strolled into town and drew a big crowd.

The new QB fired touchdown strikes of sixty-seven yards and fifty-five yards and caught the eyes of the NFL world. Dallas won the game 23-20, but a new era was launched. Blake went on to lead the Bengals to their first win of the season when he piled up 366 yards in the air against Seattle. He followed up with another victory against Houston by throwing for 354 yards.

The next season, he made the All-Pro team and led the AFC with twenty-eight touchdown passes. Blake had an opportunity to begin anew. For two years, he was the face of the Bengals and played well.

Could you use a chance to start over?

I have told you these things, so that in me you may have peace. In this world you will have trouble. But take heart! I have overcome the world.

—John 16:33

Huddle Up

Not everyone makes the right decisions. When you have a choice of what to eat for dinner or what movie to see, the consequences are minimal. But when you have to make a choice with huge ramifications, the pressure is on. Maybe you have a new job offer or an important assignment has come your way when you are already stretched with time. Or, you may just want a fresh start with the Lord.

Quick Snap

No matter what options you face, seek the Lord for His guidance. Follow His direction to help you make the right selection. Perhaps you have come through a personal storm and you are ready to accept God's joy and peace back into your heart and draw closer to Him. Here are some plays you can call:

1. Make a declaration to vow to live for the Master. This is a great way to kick off a new beginning. "If

we confess our sins, he is faithful and just and will forgive us our sins and purify us from all unrighteousness" (1 John 1:9).

2. Seek forgiveness. Ask the Lord to cleanse you from all sin, and pardon yourself as well. This is a difficult step but wipes the slate clean to help restore your relationship anew with Jesus Christ and those you love. "Whoever conceals their sins does not prosper, but the one who confesses and renounces them finds mercy" (Proverbs 28:13). Go to anyone you have wronged, apologize, and ask them to give you another chance. You might have offended a loved one or your employer. Admit what you have done with a humble heart, accept the consequences, and get busy to rebuild the trust you have lost.

3. Make restitution. "If anyone gives a neighbor silver or goods for safekeeping and they are stolen from the neighbor's house, the thief if caught, must pay back double" (Exodus 22:7).

    If you have mistreated a person, you must make amends. This does not only pertain to a thief, but to a liar, or backbiter, or to someone who has made cruel remarks. If you are guilty, seek forgiveness and set the record straight.

4. Forget the past. The famous actor John Wayne once said, "looking back is a bad habit." The devil wants to remind you of your prior sin every day. Rebuke him in Jesus's name and shove these memories aside. But don't ever forget how much your actions hurt the ones you love, and use this to motivate you to strive to make the right choices in the future.

5. Claim the victory. Our human nature leads us to make mistakes. When you know God has shown mercy on you, that is all that matters. "Brothers and sisters, I do not consider myself yet to have taken hold of it. But one thing I do: Forgetting what is behind and straining toward what is ahead" (Philippians 3:13). Learn from past wrongs and pledge to do better in the future.

Jeff Blake awed the crowd in Cincinnati when he was presented the chance to show his talents. Reach deep inside and find the gift God has given you to use for Him. Seize the opportunity He provides to you, and make the most of the day. Who Dey!

Week 22

INCREASE YOUR SPIRITUAL TEMPERATURE

Carry each other's burdens, and in this way you will fulfill the law of Christ.

—Galatians 6:2

The Freezer Bowl. January 10, 1982. The Bengals hosted San Diego in the AFC Championship game with a windchill factor of fifty-nine degrees below zero.

What tricks did the players on the offensive line have up their sleeves? None—they did not wear any. Their arms—covered in Vaseline—were exposed. The line did not wear sleeves so the defensive lineman could not grab on to them. In doing so, they sent a mental statement to the defense—We are tough and will not be intimidated.

The Bengals had mentally prepared for the game and the bitter cold. Game temperatures hovered around nine degrees below zero the entire game. San Diego's owner had asked Bengals assistant GM Mike Brown to postpone the game due to the cold. No way.

Kenny Anderson had the only hot hand that day. The MVP quarterback completed fourteen of twenty-two passes for 162 yards and two TDs as Cincinnati won the game 27-0.

Have you had times when you felt cold in the spirit? Do you want to stay "hot" for the Lord?

> *The righteous person may have many troubles, but the Lord delivers him from them all.*
>
> —Psalm 34:19

Huddle Up

Christians are normal people and can get in a rut like anyone else. Life's routines and troubles can weigh heavy on your mind at times. Football players, baseball players, athletes, and coaches can find themselves in a slump. You are no different. Life's struggles may heap burdens on you and at times you grow discouraged and cold in your walk with the Lord.

Quick Snap

Sometimes football players might mix up their routines to prepare for a game to try to break out of a slump. Others stay the course and work through their difficulties. Practice makes perfect is the mindset—a breakthrough will come. As a believer, there are some ways to keep warm in Christ and avoid any time in the freezer:

1. Engage in close fellowship. Embers keep the fire alive, and when they separate, the blaze dies. When you feel your "fire for the Lord" start to dwindle, stoke

the flames with some companionship with Christian friends. Become involved in a local charity or with a civic organization that shares your political views. God called you to help and be a light to others. Don't let your passion become dampened.

2. Toss out any bad habits. When you feel the cold chills of the enemy, slather on that Vaseline and shake them off. Walk away from the TV or pull the plug on the computer when tempted to do evil. Pray and ask the Lord to reveal your sins and convict you of all wrongdoing.

3. Find a prayer space. If you have ever tended a campfire, you know kindling and wood feed it and keep it alive. This is a continuous process. As a follower of the Gospel, you must consistently pray to keep your enthusiasm alive. When you sense the icy breath of Satan, go deep. Clean out a closet or other private area of your home and spend more time there in prayer with your heavenly Father. He will reignite the flames again.

4. Praise the Father: When you give all glory to God, you can melt the icicles of discouragement or fear around your heart. The warmth of your praise melts the coldness that may have formed from bitterness and neglect. Rejoice in the Lord!

5. Share your faith. This strengthens your commitment to God. When you tell others how good the Lord has been to you, you are accountable, and this is good. You can be an example and lead others to Christ. Stay on fire for the Lord.

Everyone gets cold once in a while. Recognize the signs and make sure you move to a warm place where you can unthaw. Adopt a game plan like the Bengals did in the "Freezer Bowl." Their strategy made success difficult for the defense. The same is true for a Christian. You must team up with God to develop a line of attack to stop the devil cold. Who Dey!

Week 23

WAIT ON YOUR BREAKTHROUGH MOMENT

You will not have to fight this battle. Take up your positions; stand firm and see the deliverance the Lord will give you, Judah and Jerusalem. Do not be afraid; do not be discouraged. Go out to face them tomorrow, and the Lord will be with you.
—2 Chronicles 20:17

The odds were against them from the kickoff. The undefeated Kansas City Chiefs rolled into Cincinnati to take on the 4-5 Bengals.

First-year coach Marvin Lewis had chosen to motivate his squad the night before and showed a clip from the movie Ali. He highlighted the portion of the film when Muhammed Ali "shocked the world" and knocked out favorite Sonny Liston to claim the title of heavyweight champion of the world. In the game the next day, an unexpected player followed suit and surprised everyone with some crucial plays that were key to the team's unanticipated victory.

Peter Warrick was a wide receiver selected by the Bengals four seasons earlier in the first round. The number-4 pick's disappointing performance had not lived up to the high hopes the franchise had for his career. But that all changed when he took matters into his own hands and delivered with two scores in the fourth quarter to help defeat Kansas City 24-19.

Warrick showcased his speed on a sixty-eight-yard punt return for a TD and later on a seventy-seven-yard touchdown strike from quarterback Jon Kitna.

He had hung on through some tough seasons hoping for this moment to arrive. But he lived up to expectations and provided the spark the team needed to "stun" the Chiefs.

Do you live the way God expects you to live? Do you want a breakthrough so you can be used by God?

> *But when he, the Spirit of truth, comes, he will guide you in all truth. He will not speak on his own; he will speak only what he hears, and he will tell you what is yet to come.*
> —John 16:13

Huddle Up

There may be instances in your life where you have grown tired of waiting on the sidelines for your opportunity. You know you possess a talent to offer the Lord. But what? How can God use you?

Quick Snap

Once you make up your mind you want to be used to glorify God, get ready and be prepared for it to happen. The call may come right away or much later. The Lord may even direct you in paths you never dreamed. Here are some suggestions to prepare you for your breakthrough moment:

1. Make sure your heart is right with God, and seek the Lord in prayer. Talk to Him on a regular and persistent basis. Don't give up. "Rejoice always, pray without ceasing" (1 Thessalonians 5:16–17 ESV).

   This does not mean to pray 24/7, but rather remain in a prayerful state of mind, and pray often. Find a special time and place for intimate conversations with your creator.

2. Sacrifice and show the Master you mean business. Take a break from an activity you enjoy or skip a few meals to fast and pray. "So we fasted and petitioned our God about this, and he answered our prayer" (Ezra 8:23).

   Be sure you do this with discretion and sincerity, and do not draw attention to yourself. This is a private commitment between you and God. Be ready to accept the answer He gives you.

3. Forgive others. Perhaps you hold a grudge against someone. This could be the key for God to use you. Cleanse your heart and spirit of any bitterness. You have a choice to forgive whether the offender deserves your mercy or not. Free yourself from the chains of anger, and accept God's peace. "Do not judge, and you will not be judged. Do not condemn, and you will not be condemned. Forgive, and you will be forgiven" (Luke 6:37).

4. Be patient. For many, this is the most difficult. Several seasons passed before Peter Warrick's breakthrough moment finally arrived. In today's drive-thru society, people want response and service NOW. God wants

you to persevere until He chooses His perfect time. He knows what He is doing. "Wait for the Lord; be strong and take heart and wait for the Lord" (Psalm 27:14).
5. Stay ready. When the time is right, He will call your name and put you into the game. Don't get caught off guard. Stay prepared and be on call to do what He asks of you. "Never be lacking in zeal, but keep your spiritual fervor, serving the Lord" (Romans 12:11).

When you follow these steps, you are better prepared for your time to shine. Just remember, it's not about you. Give Him the glory in all you do. Pray, sacrifice, forgive, wait and be ready. Who Dey!

Week 24

KEEP YOUR PROMISES

Do not be quick with your mouth, do not be hasty in your heart to utter anything before God. God is in heaven and you are on earth, so let your words be few.
—Ecclesiastes 5:2

You don't have to be a Bengals fan to know that Chad Johnson flew off at the mouth at times. He demonstrated confidence combined with brashness. But he loved attention.

Such was the case before Cincinnati played host to the undefeated Kansas City Chiefs in November 2003. The six-time Pro-Bowl receiver guaranteed a Queen City win a few days before the contest. His prophetic outlook made media headlines, and several radio sports talk shows highlighted the prediction for his team, which held a 4-5 record on the season.

But Johnson put his money where his mouth was and hauled in seven passes for seventy-four yards to help the Bengals upset the Chiefs 24-19. This particular time, Johnson's promise came true. The question is, did he use good judgment? What was his motivation?

Have you ever made a promise and backed away from your commitment?

When a man makes a vow to the Lord or takes an oath to obligate himself by a pledge, he must not break his word but must do everything he said.

—Numbers 30:2

Huddle Up

Have you ever made any of the following statements? "I'll pray for you." "I'll call you." "Let's do lunch later this week." "The check is in the mail." "We need to spend some time together." "We will do that when I get back." Do any of these questions sound familiar? After you say these things, do you follow through, or are they empty promises?

Quick Snap

Think of a time you just finished a conversation with a friend who shared his heart with you, and you end the discussion with a pledge to keep them in your prayers. Did you remember to pray? When you commit to something, you need to follow through as a believer. Your friend expects you to keep your vow, and God does too. Don't fall into the trap of uttering idle phrases you don't mean. Here are some ways to honor your word:

1. Think before you speak. When you tell someone you will call and don't, you send the wrong signal and cause people to question your character. This

can hurt your testimony. Honor your responsibilities and write them down on your calendar or set a reminder on your mobile device to help you remember. Integrity matters.
2. Mean what you say. This not only applies to your verbal conversations, but with text messages and emails. When you make a promise to spend time with your children and don't do it, you disappoint them and send the wrong message that they are not important. Keep your word so your family knows they can count on you.
3. Back up what you say with action. When you arrange to meet a friend for coffee at 8:30 a.m., be on time. Life happens, and appointments need to be rearranged on occasion, but communicate the reason. Don't make up a lie to get out of your commitments.
4. Realize the power of your words. If you break a promise to a nonbeliever, you can discourage him from seeking the Lord and because of this, hurt your witness. A Christian is a representative of heaven and must strive to be honest at all costs.

You don't have to be brash enough to predict the outcome of a game before it's played like Chad Johnson did. He and his teammates were fortunate enough to back up his claim with a win. But when it comes down to keeping your word, honor your obligation at all costs. Who Dey!

Week 25

BE STEADFAST IN YOUR JOURNEY

What is mankind that you are mindful of them, human beings that you care for them? You have made them all a little lower than the angels and crowned them with glory and honor. You made them rulers over the works of your hands; you put everything under their feet.

—Psalm 8:4–6

He is one of the most beloved Bengals of all time. Cris Collinsworth, drafted by Cincinnati in the second round in 1981, was the thirty-seventh overall pick. He played his entire eight-year NFL career for the Bengals.

As a wide receiver, he piled up four seasons with more than one thousand yards. He was named to three Pro Bowls and one first team All-Pro in 1983.

Collinsworth was a nice target at six feet five inches tall, but he had speed that made him a constant deep threat.

In Super Bowl XVI, he caught five passes for 107 yards. He finished his career in Cincinnati with 417 receptions for 6,698 yards and thirty-six touchdowns. His final game was in Super Bowl XXIII where he caught three passes for forty yards.

Now a popular NFL commentator with Monday Night Football, he always smiles and takes time to talk to people. To this day, he remains a fan favorite because of his dependability on and off the field.

Do you maintain a positive attitude in your walk with Christ? Can people depend on you in tough times?

> *You gave me life and showed me kindness, and in your providence watched over my spirit.*
>
> —Job 10:12

Huddle Up

Think of a time when your family just received some horrible news. Perhaps a loved one has a terminal illness or your spouse lost her job. Life can deal you some hard knocks and make you weary of the battle. No matter the circumstance, your loved ones or friends need you to be there for them. How will you respond? Are you steadfast and dependable?

Quick Snap

In times of crisis and uncertainty, you must be the one people can rely on to remain cool under pressure. Here are some ways to stay calm under a heavy load:

1. Pray before you react. You may not have time to pray right away in certain situations, but you can have a spirit of prayer. Speak with your heavenly Father soon. Trust in Him to comfort you and point you in the right direction. "But the advocate, the Holy

Spirit, whom the Father will send in my name, will teach you all things and will remind you of everything I have said to you" (John 14:26).
2. Talk with your pastor and seek wise counsel. He is the shepherd of the flock and should take time to discuss matters with you. Don't hesitate to reach out to your church leaders and learn from their wisdom.
3. Be accountable. Organize a small group of Christian friends and check in with each other on a regular basis. This is a fantastic way to build solid friendships and stay true. "As iron sharpens iron, so one person sharpens another" (Proverbs 27:17).
4. Look for the good in each situation. Even in times of trial, the Lord wants to teach you a life lesson. Seek the message He has for you and know He cares for you. "Finally, brothers and sisters, whatever is true, whatever is noble, whatever is right, whatever is pure, whatever is lovely, whatever is admirable—if anything is excellent or praiseworthy—think about such things" (Philippians 4:8).
5. Encourage and be a light to others. When you show a consistent reliability on God's promises, you can provide hope in dark times. Be the one your family and friends turn to when they need a lift. Pray with them, love them, and remind them of God's faithfulness. "Each of us should please our neighbors for their good, to build them up" (Romans 15:2).

Fans in Cincinnati loved Collinsworth because he was dependable, likeable, and personable. He did his job with a smile. Be committed in your walk and faith in Christ. Who Dey!

Week 26

BE HUMBLE AND GET THE JOB DONE

When pride comes, then comes disgrace, but with humility comes wisdom.

—Proverbs 11:2

Some players have already planned and rehearsed the endzone celebrations they plan to carry out following a touchdown. Excessive demonstrations have led to fines and penalties. Some celebrations have even seen fights break out where players have been injured.

Why celebrate for doing their job? Athletes are paid to score touchdowns. I never see a bank teller dance after she takes my deposit or a receptionist turn a flip after she answers the telephone.

My son's high school baseball coach always said if you hit your first home run, act like you've hit one before. Keep your head down and round the bases.

This is what fans loved about Isaac Curtis. He was drafted fifteenth overall pick in the first round by the Bengals in 1973. He had world-class speed and ran the one-hundred-yard dash in 9.3 seconds.

But Cincinnati General Manager Paul Brown most liked the attitude of the four-time Pro-Bowl honoree. Brown said the speedster had a quiet confidence about him. He described him as gentle. He did not jump up and down, spike the ball, or trash talk. He just got the job done.

In his twelve years to wear the orange and black, Curtis wrapped up 416 catches for 7,101 yards and fifty-three TDs. His remarkable 17.1 yards per catch remains a Bengals record. He was loved by Cincinnati fans for his quiet and productive demeanor.

Pride brings a person low, but the lowly in spirit gain honor.
—Proverbs 29:23

Huddle Up

Are you humble? Do you crave attention and recognition? Have you been told you need humility?

Quick Snap

In today's hustle and bustle society, you have to look out for number one. Right? Wrong. Modesty is an admirable trait to possess. Here are some ways to develop this commendable characteristic:

1. Show honesty. Don't be fake. Use the gifts God has given you, and don't pretend to be something you are not. "Wisdom's instruction is to fear the Lord, and humility comes before honor" (Proverbs 15:33).

2. Show gratitude. Make a point to thank those who help you and return the favor when you can. Never take life for granted and be thankful for God's blessings on your life. "Give thanks to the Lord, for he is good; his love endures forever" (1 Chronicles 16:34).
3. Show service to others. Don't hesitate to help someone, even if you have to go out of your way. Try your best to improve a person's situation with love and kindness. "For even the Son of Man did not come to be served, but to serve, and to give his life as a ransom for many" (Mark 10:45).
4. Show responsibility. When something goes wrong, take credit if you are at fault. Don't look to others for an excuse but stare in the mirror first. "For each one should carry their own load" (Galatians 6:5).
5. Show praise and love. Honor the Lord and show admiration to the one who saved you. Raise your hands, and give thanks to your creator. All praise and glory go to the Master. "Praise the Lord, my soul; all my inmost being, praise his holy name" (Psalm 103:1).

When you get out of the way and make room for the Lord, you will be blessed. Isaac Curtis never taunted other players or celebrated his athletic accomplishments in front of his colleagues. He did what he was supposed to do, and he excelled. Players, coaches, and fans respected number 85. Who Dey!

Week 27

ESTABLISH AND ENFORCE THE RULES

As the Father has loved me, so have I loved you. Now remain in my love.

—John 15:9

Isaac Curtis was a nightmare for other teams to defend. His lightning-fast speed left cornerbacks and safeties in the dust with no answer for him. Number 85 ran the hundred-yard dash in 9.3 seconds and the two-hundred-meter dash in 20.7 seconds. He was a Pro Bowl selection four times in his career.

His opponents tried to double- and triple-team him at times to slow him down.

In 1973, Cincinnati won the Central Division and matched up with Miami. The Dolphins, who went on later to win the Super Bowl, devised a plan to slow him down. Their defensive backs pushed, shoved, and bumped him while he ran his route. This caught on, and other teams started to use the same strategy. Paul Brown complained to the NFL's Competition Committee that his wide receiver could not perform under these circumstances.

Thus the "Isaac Curtis rule" was hatched. The rule states that a defender is allowed to make contact with the receiver within the first five yards of the line of scrimmage. Any contact after that is considered holding and a penalty.

Curtis changed the game. Have you established boundaries on your home field?

> *With my whole heart I seek you; let me not wander from your commandments!*
>
> —Psalm 119:10 ESV

Huddle Up

You must have guidelines for your home. Just like any locker room or athletic organization, the rules must be clear and enforced and are put in place to protect the players, make the competition fair, and provide for good conduct. Without rules, there is chaos—they are established in all aspects of life: sports, government, and in the workplace. The Bible clearly establishes God's commandments to live by in your daily life. If you do not follow His instructions, you give Satan the opportunity to set chaos and destruction in motion. Follow the rules! If you don't, the penalties will lead to heartbreak and harm and keep you from receiving the blessings God has planned for you.

Quick Snap

In Matthew 7:12, Jesus established the Golden Rule in which He admonished us to treat others the way we wish to be treated. This speaks volumes, but there are some other principles you must also set for your loved ones:

1. Show respect and honor. Without these, rules hold no value. Do not be a tyrant, and yell and shout. Instead, be stern yet gentle. You have to show respect to get it. "Be devoted one to another in love. Honor one another above yourselves" (Romans 12:10).
2. Attend church together. Take your family to church on a regular basis and worship with them. Set the standard and be the example. If there is rebellion, enforce the rules. You are the head of the home. "My son, keep your father's command and do not forsake your mother's teaching" (Proverbs 6:20).
3. Spend time together. You may have church, ballgames, and school functions to attend, but make special time to go out together as a team. Go to a family-friendly movie, or take a trip to a museum or amusement park. When you spend time with your kids, you show them how important they are. "The father of a righteous child has great joy; a man who fathers a wise son rejoices in him" (Proverbs 23:24).
4. Carry out the orders. If you do not enforce your own laws, why have them? Establish consequences and don't back down. Do not give third and fourth chances. Once a rule is broken, administer the punishment. You might not want to do this, but if you don't, your children never learn to respect your authority or anyone else's. "Whoever spares the rod, hates their children, but the one who loves their children is careful to discipline them" (Proverbs 13:24).
5. Help, defend, and encourage one another. Let them know you want the best for them. Accept them for who they are in the Lord, and do what is necessary

to protect them. "Fathers, do not exasperate your children; instead bring them up in the training and instruction of the Lord" (Ephesians 6:4).

When you model godly leadership in the home, you also teach your kids to become leaders. There may be power struggles along the way, but put the Lord first, and the defense has no chance to guard you. Who Dey!

Week 28

BRING JOY TO OTHERS

Be joyful in hope, patient in affliction, faithful in prayer.
—Romans 12:12

From 1971 to 1986, Cincinnati fans had a love affair with Kenny Anderson. He was a crowd favorite because of the way he played the game and treated his devotees. He interacted with the fans and always signed autographs. He never shied away from his supporters and treated people with respect. But above all, he played hard and that is what they liked most about him.

Before the start of the 2017 NFL off-season, per Wikipedia, he held at least thirty-one Bengals franchise records, which included:

- **Completions:** career (2,654), game (40 on 12-20-1982 against San Diego), playoffs (110), playoff season (53 in 1981)
- **Pass Attempts:** career (4,475), playoffs (166), playoff season (77 in 1981)

- **Passing Yards:** career (32,838), playoffs (1,321), playoff season (653 in 1981), playoff game (354 on 1-9-1983 against the New York Jets)
- **Passing TDs:** career (197), playoffs (9), playoff season (5 in 1981), playoff game (2 on 1-9-1983 against the New York Jets, with Boomer Esiason)
- **Interceptions:** career (160), season (22 in 1978, with Boomer Esiason, Jon Kitna), playoffs (6), playoff season (3 in 1982, with Boomer Esiason, Andy Dalton), playoff game (3 on 1-9-1983 against the New York Jets, with Andy Dalton)
- **Passer Rating:** playoffs (93.5)
- **Sacks:** career (398), season (46 in 1979, with Andy Dalton), playoff game (5 on 1-24-1982, with Boomer Esiason)
- **Yards/Pass Attempts:** playoffs (7.96), playoff season (10.11 in 1982), playoff game (10.11 on 1-9-1983 against the New York Jets)
- **Pass Yards/Game:** season (277.2 in 1982), playoffs (220.2), playoff season (354 in 1982)
- **300+ Yard Passing Games:** playoffs (2)

Anderson was the 1981 MVP of the league and offensive player of the year. He appeared in four Pro Bowls and twice led the NFL in passing. He was a joy for Bengals fans. His accomplishments brought smiles to the Cincinnati fans all the time, and the crowds poured into the stadium to witness him give 100 percent every game.

Do you bring joy to those around you? When you come home, is your family happy to see you?

Your statutes are my heritage forever; they are the joy of my heart.
—Psalm 119:111

Huddle Up

Ask yourself: Are you content? This does not mean you must ignore troubles you encounter on a daily basis or turn a deaf ear to world issues like terrorism or natural disasters. But you can have joy no matter what circumstances life throws at you.

Quick Snap

Here are some strategies to maintain delight in the Lord:

1. Praise God in all aspects. There is a positive side to most situations, even though you may not see the good immediately. Of course you grieve if a loved one passes, and you are disappointed if you lose your job, but know the Lord will watch out for you and carry you through to the other side. "God is spirit, and his worshipers must worship in the Spirit and in truth" (John 4:24).
2. Keep a daily journal. Take a few minutes, gather your thoughts, and write them down. This can provide a temporary distraction to a negative situation and a private outlet to express your innermost sentiments. Or you can use this to capture the moments of blessing and answered prayers in your life. Go back and review your notes on a regular basis, and focus on the positive.

3. Make a point to smile and encourage others. A "thank you" or "have a nice day" can go a long way to lift others.
4. Know God has a plan for you. Be patient and look ahead at the great things the Lord has in store for you. Don't force the issues, but be ready for Him to say, "let's go." "Many are the plans in a person's heart, but it is the Lord's purpose that prevails" (Proverbs 19:21).
5. Show God's love to everyone around you. When you do this with a smile and in kindness, you can be an inspiration to all you meet. "For I am not ashamed of the gospel, because it is the power of God that brings salvation to everyone who believes: first to the Jew, then the Gentile" (Romans 1:16).

Strive to be productive and demonstrate an upbeat attitude. You can spread joy in all you do. Be glad you are a child of the King, and don't be afraid to brighten someone's day. Who Dey!

Week 29

ANTICIPATE THE PASS

Can a man walk on hot coals without his feet being scorched?
—Proverbs 6:28

David Fulcher was the ideal safety. He had size, speed, and ferocity. In 1998, he hauled in five interceptions, scored a touchdown, and earned an appearance in the Pro Bowl. He helped to guide the Bengals to a 12-4 season record and a trip to Super Bowl XXIII.

Fulcher, selected in the third round, said the Super Bowl was the greatest game he ever played. He made several important tackles, recorded a sack, and forced a fumble to give his team the ball.

The next season, he played even better. The six-foot-three safety from Los Angeles picked off eight passes and tied a Cincinnati single-season record with three picks in one game. He was selected to another Pro Bowl for his performance.

In 1990, he continued to be a productive defensive player. He made his third straight Pro Bowl team, snagged four interceptions, and recorded fifty-three solo tackles. Fulcher was a force to be reckoned with and never backed down from a challenge. His anticipation skills were among the best ever seen from a defensive safety.

Interceptions upset the opponent's strategy. The devil is always attempting a play that will take you down. Do you intercept temptation when it comes your way? Do you see evil when it approaches and resist, or do you give way to the devil? What do you do that will turn the play around?

When tempted, no one should say, "God is tempting me." For God cannot be tempted by evil, nor does he tempt anyone.
—James 1:13

Huddle Up

Satan is aware of your humanity. He knows your weaknesses and how to seize on them at the right time. Temptation is "a desire to do something, especially wrong or unwise" and comes in many forms. You know when you have sinned because the Holy Spirit pricks your conscience and burdens your heart with conviction. But there are ways to intercept the traps of the devil and save your team from defeat.

Quick Snap

You are not alone in this battle. The forces of evil are active and work to destroy you. Here are some suggestions to fight the relentless battle against the enemy:

1. Recognize: The devil uses many tricks. He knows your vulnerabilities and does not play fair. You might wrestle with carnal passions, but the first step to

restrain the sin is to recognize it and anticipate the throw, just like David Fulcher did as a safety. "On reaching the place, he said to them, 'Pray that you will not fall into temptation'" (Luke 22:40).

2. Resist: "Submit yourselves, then, to God. Resist the devil, and he will flee from you" (James 4:7). Each time you say no, you become stronger. When you give in, you become weak and a larger target for Satan's quarterback.

3. Run: Flee from what tempts you. When you waddle in the pigpen, you get muddy. You must gain strength in order to combat the forces of evil. Only Satan coaxes you to do wrong—the Lord will not tempt you. "Reject every kind of evil" (1 Thessalonians 5:22). You are no match for the devil because he throws all he has at you to try to make you fail. If you are a recovered alcoholic, stay away from the bars. If you are addicted to lust, avoid the internet or install family-friendly filters. Stay away from what tempts you. Focus on an interest that involves a network of believers who draw you closer to God.

4. Reinforce: The best place to go when tempted is to God. No matter the circumstance, you must ask the Lord for help. Call upon God and fellow Christians for reinforcements and backup. "And I will do whatever you ask in my name, so that the Father may be glorified in the Son" (John 14:13). You must admit you are weak in order to become stronger. Form a group of male friends to hold you accountable and call on them in times of crisis.

5. Remain: Stay in the Word of God and use the armor the Lord has provided to you. Memorize scripture and quote it aloud when Satan attacks, and speak the name of Jesus.

When you intercept Satan's advances, you place your family and friends in a better position to be victorious. Don't let a single pass get by you. Be on the defense and defeat temptation. Who Dey!

Week 30

YOU CAN BE BOLD

When I called, you answered me; you gently emboldened me.
—Psalm 138:3

Bob Trumpy was known for his confidence. Although he was drafted in the 12th round by the Bengals, he had a strong work ethic. The two-time Pro Bowl tight end had a blue-collar reputation.

He earned a starting spot his rookie year and had thirty-seven receptions for 639 yards and three scores. In 1970, he enjoyed his best season as a pro football player. He hauled in thirty-seven passes for 835 yards for a franchise record of 22.6 yards per catch. He tossed in nine touchdowns. Over his career in Cincinnati, he totaled 4,600 yards in the air and averaged 15.4 yards per catch with thirty-five TDs.

But he is best known for his broadcast career. He worked for NBC and called Monday Night Football and two Super Bowls. He also worked for CBS and had a long and successful sports talk show on WLW radio in Cincinnati.

He was named the 2014 recipient of the Pete Rozelle Radio-Television Award, a lifetime achievement presented by the Pro Football Hall of Fame for "longtime exceptional contributions to radio and television in professional football."

Trumpy is well-known for his self-assurance on the air. He never backed down from his point of view and always backed up what he said. Some considered his manner to be arrogant, but many respected his preparation and boldness.

Are you a confident Christian? You can be.

Therefore, since we have such a hope, we are very bold.
—2 Corinthians 3:12

Huddle Up

God does not expect you to be a meek believer and let people walk all over you. You have a right to stand in pride if you are a child of the King. Have you been labeled weak because you stand up against sin?

Quick Snap

There is a difference between confidence and cockiness. Bold faith does not require you to be loud and obnoxious. In fact, true Christian men often serve God with quiet confidence. Below are some traits of a bold Christian. Do any apply to you?

1. You depend on the Holy Spirit to keep you from evil. Avoid all desire to take part in an act that might disrupt your journey of faith and hurt you and your loved ones.
2. You abstain from sin. You flee from temptation and wrong choices. Live so close to God that His spirit

alerts you anytime you even come close to a bad decision.
3. You love others. You demonstrate a genuine love for your family, friends, brothers and sisters in Christ, and lost souls.
4. You pray and read God's Word on a regular basis. You cherish your daily time spent with your heavenly Father.
5. You have a true desire for the things of God. You have the most fun when you serve alongside God's people in Christian fellowship.
6. You are burdened for lost souls. You show genuine concern for those who are without the Lord and ask God for opportunities to witness to them about His love.
7. You praise and glorify God. Worship Him and magnify His holy name for He is worthy of our love, devotion, and gratitude.
8. You serve others. When you help those in need, you are following God's commands.
9. You examine yourself. Never take your salvation for granted. Always look inside to see if there is more you can do for Him.
10. You lead your family. You should not be satisfied until you know your loved ones are ready for heaven. Do your best to show them the way of the cross.

Be confident in your relationship with Christ, and leave no room for people to question your salvation. Be bold so others will notice and long for the same peace and satisfaction you have. Never back down from your faith. Who Dey!

Week 31

STAY ON THE SAME TEAM

The Spirit clearly says that in later times some will abandon the faith and follow deceiving spirits and things taught by demons.

—1 Timothy 4:1

Louis Breeden was a popular Bengal and was selected in the seventh round of the 1977 NFL Draft.

After he missed his rookie season due to an injury, he was ready to play. He became a starter and made an instant impact on the team in 1978. As a cornerback, he picked off three passes and recovered two fumbles. Two years later, he led the team with seven interceptions.

In 1981, he set a team record when he picked off a pass from Dan Fouts and took it back 102 yards for a touchdown. The Bengals went on that day to defeat San Diego 40-17. The interception return remains a franchise record, tied with a similar play made by Artrell Hawkins.

Breeden spent his entire career in the NFL in the Queen City and retired in 1987. Over his ten-year span in the league, he totaled 33 interceptions for 558 yards and two touchdowns.

He was a fan favorite of Cincinnati because of his play on the field and his dedication to the team.

Hopefully, you want to stay on the Lord's team forever. We all want to be on a squad we know wins in the end. But it's easy for people to drift away.

And may your hearts be fully committed to the Lord our God, to live by his decrees and obey his commands, as at this time.

—1 Kings 8:61

Huddle Up

Have you noticed yourself on the bench more often lately? Did you take a time out from prayer and the Word of God? God's caution signs can slip up on you if you are not careful. Pay attention to those warnings so you can identify the problem before it becomes too big.

Quick Snap

You have noticed these negative traits creep up on you? It's time to nip them in the bud. Here are some tips to help you stay on the Lord's Super Bowl Championship team forever:

1. Take regular inventory. If you are serious about your walk with God, examine your faith often. This can be done when you attend church or through your prayer and devotions. "It does not dishonor others, it is not self-seeking, it is not easily angered, it keeps no record of wrongs" (1 Corinthians 13:5).

2. Get back on the road when you notice yourself begin to drift. There are no rumble strips, but there are signals of danger. Perhaps you justify reasons to skip church, you "forget" to pray or read God's Word, or you may not feel His presence anymore. "See to it, brothers and sisters, that none of you has a sinful, unbelieving heart that turns away from the living God" (Hebrews 3:12).
3. Pray each day for forgiveness and guidance. You are human and will sin. But the Father forgives and instructs. "If we confess our sins, he is faithful and just and will forgive us our sins and purify us from all unrighteousness" (1 John 1:9). This does not give you a green light to continue to repeat the cycle of sin and forgiveness. You must mean business when you ask for God's pardon and determine to be faithful and true.
4. Stay true to your faith, even in the storm. When tough times come, you must not abandon your comforter. Hold on to His hand, and never doubt He loves you and takes care of you. "You will be hated by everyone because of me, but the one who stands firm to the end will be saved" (Matthew 10:22). Know the reward is worth the fight.
5. Remember, this is a marathon, not a sprint. Run the race to win. There are times when you have to slow down and pace yourself, but know there is a prize when you cross the ribbon. "Do you not know that in a race all the runners run, but only one gets the prize? Run in such a way as to get the prize" (1 Corinthians 9:24).

Set a goal to remain on the victorious team until the end. There are no trade clauses unless you ask for one. Have the determination to stay on the Lord's side for the entire game. Who Dey!

Week 32

BE WILLING TO DO WHAT GOD WANTS

"For I know the plans I have for you," declares the Lord, "plans to prosper you and not to harm you, plans to give you hope and a future."

—Jeremiah 29:11

Andrew Whitworth did everything he was asked to do. Cincinnati selected him in 2006 in the second round of the NFL Draft. He soon found a spot on special teams and was moved to left guard in his second game as a rookie.

In a contest against Cleveland, he helped the Bengals' ground game to gain 481 yards. From that point on, he became a regular starter.

Then against San Diego, he spearheaded the offensive line, which produced a season-high 545 yards on the ground. He also had a key block on a Rudi Johnson seven-yard touchdown run.

But in 2009, Coach Marvin Lewis moved Whitworth from guard to left tackle. In all sixteen games he started, he gave up no more than five sacks. His big day came on December 12, 2010, when he caught a one-yard touchdown pass from quarterback Carson Palmer against Pittsburgh. The TD was his first career score, and he became the first Bengal offensive lineman to catch a touchdown pass since 1995.

The 2014 season proved to be his best. He did not allow any sacks from his position and his quarterback, Andy Dalton, was only hit one time. He embraced the move to another position to help his team.

Would you be willing to move to a new position if God called you there? Are you open to God's will for your life?

This is good, and pleases God our Savior.

—1 Timothy 2:3

Huddle Up

What is God's plan for you? Have you placed limits on the Lord, or are you open to change?

Quick Snap

Maybe you have taught Sunday School for years, and now the Lord wants you to give it up for another ministry. Maybe you have wanted to sing, but He wants you to write. How can you be certain of God's design for your life? Here are some factors to help you be obedient when He calls you:

1. Walk with God. Allow Him to lead you and follow in His steps. Be patient and give Him control. Take the time to be alone with God. Maybe you have a prayer closet or you can take a walk in the park—just you and Him. "In all your ways submit to him, and he will make your paths straight" (Proverbs 3:6).

2. Listen to Him. The Lord does not give you instructions until He knows you are in tune with him and have a willing attitude. He may not want you to go on a mission trip, but He wants you to surrender your heart if He asks. "Therefore, I urge you, brothers and sister, in view of God's mercy, to offer your bodies as a living sacrifice, holy and pleasing to God—this is your true and proper worship" (Romans 12:1).
3. Do not fight or resist. There is no way to negotiate with God and win. Once you are open to His direction, your heart is at peace. "I desire to do your will, my God; your law is within my heart" (Psalm 40:8).
4. Seek wise counsel. You might want to talk with your pastor or a close Christian friend who has gone through a similar situation. Ask them to pray with you, and learn from their experience. "For lack of guidance a nation falls, but victory is won through many advisers" (Proverbs 11:14).
5. Trust and obey. After God has told you what He wants you to do, believe He is able to see you through. He does not put you in a situation to fail, and He equips you with the tools you need for any task He assigns. "Do not merely listen to the word, and so deceive yourselves. Do what it says" (James 1:22).

When you find God's plan for your life, you experience excitement and uneasiness at the same time, but put your trust in Him and get to work! Andrew Whitworth changed positions for the betterment of the team. Be flexible so God can use you for the glory of the kingdom. Who Dey!

Week 33

DON'T PAY THE COST

For even the Son of Man did not come to be served, but to serve, and to give his life as a ransom for many.
—Mark 10:45

There has never been a more perfect definition of a linebacker than Reggie Williams. The Bengals drafted him in 1976 in the third round. He played his entire NFL career in Cincinnati and appeared in Super Bowls XVI and XXIII.

He recorded sixteen interceptions and twenty-three fumble recoveries, still a franchise record today. During his career, Williams piled up 62.5 sacks, the second most in the team's history. In his final two seasons, he was appointed to an open seat on the Cincinnati City Council (in 1988), then was elected for a second term (in 1989) on the Charter Party ticket.

His numerous honors include NFL All-Rookie Team (1976), the Byron "Whizzer" White Award for Humanitarian Service (1985), and the NFL Walter Payton Man of the Year Award (1986). He was also named Co-Sportsman of the Year in 1987 by Sports Illustrated.

However, he paid a price for his success with his health by playing most of his career on a bad right knee. He has undergone countless surgeries and knee replacements, which led to several infections.

He was diagnosed in 2008 with osteomyelitis, an infection of the bone, and underwent eight additional surgeries. Without the proper care, he faces the risk of amputation of his right leg, which is almost a full three inches shorter than his left. Was his success worth the pain he now endures? That's a good question. But a greater question is: How do the decisions you make today affect your future? Will they cause you eternal pain or will you live in joy and contentment because of your choices?

> *What then? Shall we sin because we are not under the law but under grace? By no means!*
>
> —Romans 6:15

Huddle Up

You face choices every day. What to wear, what to eat for lunch, what stocks to buy or sell, etc. But what about choices that lead to immorality? Every day, temptations come your way. You need to decide whether to give in to the pressure and to consider the monumental impacts to your eternal destiny.

Quick Snap

Sin always takes you farther than you want to go and hurts those you love. When you are tempted to do wrong, take these end results into account:

Don't Pay the Cost

1. Sin robs you of joy and peace. Satan's false promises can entice you to give in to his persuasion, but don't give up your long-term happiness for temporary satisfaction. Look to God for divine strength to refute evil. "You make known to me the path of life; you will fill me with joy in your presence, with eternal pleasure at your right hand" (Psalm 16:11).
2. Sin leads you down a path of destruction. You may not realize this until it's too late to turn back. Satan wants to give you more than a late hit. He wants to give you a career-ending injury.
3. Sin has the potential to ruin your profession. You read every day about circumstances that lead people to resign or face termination for an act that happened in the past. Make the right choices today to escape the pain of the future. "Do not be deceived: God cannot be mocked. A man reaps what he sows" (Galatians 6:7).
4. Sin can break up your family. The home is a direct target of the devil. He works hard to destroy the home because he knows how critical families are to the church and to peace and stability in our nation. Many of the ills of our society have a direct link to the breakdown of this important institution.

You are better than the plans Satan has to wreck your future. Think about the sorrow that awaits you if you don't repent and follow the Lord. What is worth the danger of losing your life and your soul? Nothing! Sack the devil. Who Dey!

Week 34

BE A TRUE FRIEND

Greater love has no one than this: to lay down one's life for one's friend.

—John 15:13

Mike Zimmer found out just how many true friends he had. On October 11, 2009, he coached with a broken heart. His son, daughter, and father were in the stands at Paul Brown Stadium to watch the Bengals take on Baltimore. His wife, Vikki, was not. She had unexpectedly passed away seventy-two hours before the game at age fifty of natural causes.

He needed his team to back him up, and they did not disappoint. As Cincinnati's defensive coordinator, he designed a plan to help them stop the high-powered Ravens' offense. The Bengals won 17-14 in an emotional game.

Carson Palmer connected with wide receiver Andre Caldwell for a twenty-yard TD with twenty-two seconds left in the game to propel them to the win. The defense was spectacular. They held Baltimore to eight of eleven third-down plays and shut down Derrick Mason, the team's best receiver.

When the game ended, television cameras caught Zimmer surrounded by his players on the sidelines with hugs of support. In the locker room, coach Marvin Lewis presented him with the game ball. It was a true demonstration of friendship and love.

Are you a true friend? Are you there when it counts? How have you demonstrated God's love to someone in need?

And he has given us this command: Anyone who loves God must also love their brother and sister.

—1 John 4:21

Huddle Up

Think of a time you received a desperate plea from a friend who was in need. Perhaps he asked to meet with you right away because something terrible had happened. Meanwhile you were on the twelfth hole of play in one of the best golf rounds of your life. What was your choice? Were you the hands and feet of Christ in that moment? Or did selfishness win over?

Quick Snap

Do you make yourself available, if possible, when a friend calls upon you? Do you rally around a family member in a time of crisis? Do you consider it a nuisance or a privilege to show compassion to others? Here are some characteristics of a true supporter.

1. A friend shows selfless sacrifice. Model the same love Jesus has for you. If you have to leave a golf game

early, so what? When you value your companion's concerns above your own, you do the right thing in the eyes of God.
2. A friend forgives. Despite disappointments, be quick to pardon and do not hold grudges. "A friend loves at all times, and a brother is born for adversity" (Proverbs 17:17 ESV).
3. A friend encourages. If a monumental event takes place in the life of your pal, be genuinely happy and proud for him. Don't be jealous, but be happy for his success. Be his biggest cheerleader and rejoice in his victory.
4. A friend confronts wrong and holds others accountable. If you see a buddy do wrong, talk to him in love and not in a spirit of condemnation. Listen to all sides and be supportive but stern if needed and tell him the truth. There may be a time when he has to have the same honest talk with you. "Two are better than one, because they have a good return for their labor: If either of them falls down, one can help the other up. But pity anyone who falls and has no one to help them up" (Ecclesiastes 4:9–10).
5. A friend prays for and with you. A prayer partner makes the best confidant. There is no stronger friendship than one bonded by the love of Christ.

Mike Zimmer's defense was there for him at his lowest time. The players rallied around him and gave him their best. They fought for him and won the game to show how much they cared. Mission accomplished. Who Dey!

Week 35

GIVE BACK TO YOUR COMMUNITY

Finally, all of you, be like-minded, be sympathetic, love one another, be compassionate and humble.

—1 Peter 3:8

Andy Dalton does a great job as quarterback of the Cincinnati Bengals. He was drafted in the second round in 2011. He and receiver A. J. Green have become a legitimate All-Pro combination. The two have broken NFL records for completions and yards by a rookie duo.

Dalton is one of six QBs in NFL history to throw for more than three thousand yards in each of his first three seasons. (Note: The other five are Peyton Manning, Ryan Tannehill, Andrew Luck, Cam Newton, and Russell Wilson.)

He holds many franchise records in Cincinnati, which include most yards passed, and greatest number of TDs in one season. While these numbers are important, Andy's first love is the Andy & Jordan Dalton Foundation. He considers this organization to be his ministry.

The couple started their work at local Cincinnati hospitals with children who are ill or have special needs. Their ultimate goal is to bring a smile to children's faces but continue to help families in any way possible. The Daltons know God has blessed them with a golden opportunity and want these families to feel the same way.

The foundation raises money and awareness, but the greatest goal is to help children and their parents. The group gives back to the community in a big Who Dey way. Can you do more to be a light for Christ and sacrifice your time and money to help others?

And over all these virtues put on love, which binds them together in perfect unity.

—Colossians 3:14

Huddle Up

Every day, you are surrounded by people with needs. Perhaps there is a homeless man who stand on the corner every day and holds a cardboard sign, or maybe you know a family in need of a hot meal. Think of how you can be God to them in everyday interactions.

Quick Snap

The time is now for you to act. Get involved in your area, and provide help and inspiration to those who are down and out. You are called upon to help. Financial contributions are admirable, but also consider a donation of your time and make an investment of love. Here are some reasons why you should put on the hat of charity:

1. To encourage: When you become involved, you meet other people you may not know. God presents you with the opportunity to share your faith with a new crowd and make friends at the same time. "And let us consider how we may spur one another on toward love and good deeds, not giving up meeting together, as some are in the habit of doing, but encouraging one another—and all the more as you see the Day approaching" (Hebrews 10:24–25).
2. To help: You may find yourself in a position to reach out and help a person get back on his feet. Lend a hand with trust and humility. The door is open for you to share the good news of Christ, the best assistance you can ever provide.
3. To enjoy: When you join together with like-minded people to spread joy to others, this leads to a gratifying experience. Christians can have fun while they reach others with the love of God and work together to improve their community. "How good and pleasant it is when God's people live together in unity!" (Psalm 133:1).

Now that we have established why it is important to be active in your community, here are some suggestions for places and organizations you can contact to ask how to get involved:

1. A homeless shelter
2. A pro-life organization or crisis pregnancy center
3. Local youth sports
4. After-school program

5. Local humane society
6. A writer's group
7. Hospital or hospice facility
8. Food pantry, food bank, or soup kitchen
9. Local politics
10. Christmas gifts program

These are just a few recommendations. When you become serious, do your own research and find a way to give back to your local region. When you do, you feel like you connected with A. J. Green for an eighty-nine-yard TD strike. Who Dey!

Week 36

KICK THE ENEMY THROUGH THE UPRIGHTS

No, in all these things we are more than conquerors through him who loved us.
—Romans 8:37

Jim Breech made his mark as a Bengal. He was a kicker for the team for thirteen seasons and had a 71.4 percent success rate. He made 243 out of 340 field goal tries. On extra points, he connected on 517 of 539 attempts (95.9 percent).

He scored 1,151 points for Cincinnati, a franchise record, and he is second all-time in scores in 186 consecutive games.

Breech, who wore a size five shoe, played in two Super Bowls and was nine of eleven in post-season field goal attempts. In Super Bowl XXIII, he accounted for ten of the team's sixteen points. One statistic that shines above the rest is his perfection in overtime periods. He made all nine attempts when called upon in OT.

Do you live a victorious life? Does the devil kick you around? How can you defeat evil?

In addition to all this, take up the shield of faith, with which you can extinguish all the flaming arrows of the evil one.
—Ephesians 6:16

Huddle Up

All Christians face struggles, but do you let them consume you and keep you from victory in Christ? You can break free from the chains that bind you.

Quick Snap

Life has many difficult moments. But as a believer, you can overcome them and still have joy. Your problems may not leave right away, but you can have peace in the midst of the storm. Here are some ways to enjoy your Christian journey while you wait:

1. Rise early and spend time with God. Make time each day to give your first few minutes to the Lord before you get distracted by responsibilities. "In the morning, Lord, you hear my voice; in the morning I lay my requests before you and wait expectantly" (Psalm 5:3). No matter when you rise, cast your cares and burdens before Him. What a great way to begin your day—worry free.
2. Take a few moments during the day to reflect upon God's grace and give Him thanks. In particular, this is good to do in the middle of a busy schedule. When you are always on the go, you may find it easy to relegate God to second or third place in your life. "The

Lord has done it this very day; let us rejoice today and be glad" (Psalm 118:24). Find time to show gratitude to God and brighten your day.

3. Claim authority. Do not let the devil control your situation. The Word of God and prayer are useful weapons to fight him off. Another handy tool is to rebuke Satan in the name of the Master. Give him the kick in the pants he deserves, and he will flee from you. Use the power of Christ to claim the victory.

4. Take comfort and refuge in His Word. Commit to read the Bible each day, and identify verses to memorize and quote in the midst of turmoil to give you the strength, peace, and comfort you need at the right moment. Just like Breech, the Lord is perfect in all overtime sessions against the devil.

5. Remember who wins the game. We have hope because we already know God's team comes out on top at the end of life's battle. You may encounter disappointment and discouragement at times, but look ahead to the fourth quarter when the game clock begins to wind down. You are the victor. Circumstances might look bleak, but God kicks the winning field goal as time expires. "He seized the dragon, that ancient serpent, who is the devil, or Satan, and bound him for a thousand years" (Revelation 20:2).

You don't have to be a big man to fight the forces of evil. Jim Breech was a successful kicker and stood five foot six inches tall. David defeated the giant Goliath because of His faith in God. You too can profess the Lord Jesus Christ and live a victorious life through His might. Who Dey!

Week 37

BE A VALUABLE MEMBER OF GOD'S TEAM

Look at the birds of the air; they do not sow or reap or store away in barns, and yet your heavenly Father feeds them. Are you not much more valuable than they?

—Matthew 6:26

Dave Lapham was not your ordinary offensive lineman for the Bengals. From 1974 to 1983, he anchored the front five. He played all five line positions throughout his career, which made him a valuable member of the team. His versatility and attitude demonstrated a sacrifice to do whatever was asked of him to be successful.

In 1981, he helped lead his team to the AFC championship game and an appearance in Super Bowl XVI.

For the past thirty years, he stayed connected with Cincinnati in the role of a radio commentator and TV host. His relentless support of the Bengals on the air has made him a lovable figure for decades.

His unique angles from the position of player, commentator, and fan make him an icon in the Queen City area.

Do you see the worth inside you as a child of God?

Arise, shine, for your light has come, and the glory of the Lord rises upon you.

—Isaiah 60:1

Huddle Up

Perhaps you are not involved in church or community events like some other people are. This is OK—you don't have to be. These activities are great to be involved in, but maybe this is not your style. Perhaps you prefer to do things for God that no one sees or knows about, which is a wonderful sign of humility. But no matter what you do for the kingdom, there are times when Satan attempts to make you feel worthless.

Quick Snap

Everyone is precious in the sight of God, and His love for us is unconditional. The Lord loves to see His children be faithful and follow these basic fundamentals to present His love every day to a world hungry for the gospel:

1. Show respect to others. Extend love to all people, regardless of their race, sex, religion, nationality, or their beliefs. There is no place in the family of God for bigotry. The Master depends on you to love others the same way He loves you. "The second is this: 'Love your neighbor as yourself.' There is no commandment greater than these" (Mark 12:31).
2. Show honesty. Integrity is essential to your Christian walk. The world sets a high bar of expectation for God's children to be truthful in all matters, and if

you're not, you leave room for others to question not only your salvation but God's entire plan. Show them you serve a God who is real. "To do what is right and just is more acceptable to the Lord than sacrifice" (Proverbs 21:3).

3. Show humility. A boastful or arrogant attitude can also harm your witness and be destructive to your journey. Put God first, lift up others second, and place yourself last. "When pride comes, then comes disgrace, but with humility comes wisdom" (Proverbs 11:2).

4. Show virtue. Be just and moral. You are an ambassador for the cause of Christ, and if you say one thing and do another, you risk harm to your salvation, your Christian reputation, and your relationships with others. You are counted on to be a righteous and holy representative for God, and if you hide immoral secrets, someday your sin will catch up to you, lead to humiliation and disappointment, and turn others away from the cross. Your life should be an open book with no regrets or reservations. When you have to cover something up, you need to rethink the possible consequences and whether or not you continue. Ask God for strength to stay inside the boundaries of His commandments. "So then, the law is holy, and the commandment is holy, righteous and good" (Romans 7:12).

5. Show praise to the Lord. Demonstrate your gratefulness to the Master. Don't be afraid to give thanks to the Lord in church and even in public. After all, you

rise to your feet and shout with excitement when the Bengals score a touchdown. You can do the same in your everyday life. If others observe God answer a prayer for you, seize on the opportunity to publicly acknowledge Christ, the giver of all blessings. He is worthy of your praise. "Give thanks to the Lord, for he is good; his love endures forever" (1 Chronicles 16:34).

When you use these examples to display holiness to others, you show you are a team player who is willing to play all positions. You don't need recognition, you just need God. Show Him to the world. Who Dey!

Week 38

DEVELOP YOUR SKILLS AND TALENTS

For we are God's handiwork, created in Christ Jesus to do good work, which God prepared in advance for us to do.
—Ephesians 2:10

You may know A. J. Green is one of the best receivers in Bengals history. Before the 2017 season, he hauled in 481 passes for 7,135 yards in regular contests, he posted a 14.9 yards-per-catch average and scored forty-nine touchdowns. In four playoff appearances, he caught eighteen passes for 232 yards for a 12.9 average.

His speed, toughness, and hand-eye coordination have become his trademark. He has been named to seven Pro Bowls and is a two-time All-Pro Team member.

But you may not be aware he is an accomplished juggler. He learned this skill in the second grade and has developed it over the years. At a young age, Green could handle up to four items at a time and was a member of his elementary school's juggling team.

This unique skill came in handy to help make him one of the NFL's most prolific wide receivers. Do you have a special talent you can use for the Lord?

> *Every good and perfect gift is from above, coming down from the Father of the heavenly lights, who does not change like shifting shadows.*
>
> —James 1:17

Huddle Up

You may have a hidden talent or gift you can use to honor His name. Have you ever thought to use your ability to minister for Christ?

Quick Snap

There are many ways you can use your hobbies or extracurricular activities to serve God and others. You can be a Christian example and do something you enjoy at the same time. But make sure you pray to God first and ask Him to confirm this ministry is part of His plan, and be ready to walk through the doors he opens for you. Here are some examples of talents you can use to magnify the Lord:

1. Singing. If the Lord has given you gifts to sing and/or play a musical instrument, then use them to bless others. You might offer to serve in the choir or lead the music in children's church or Vacation Bible

School. Or you may expand beyond the church doors to volunteer to minister to elderly who live in nursing homes or assisted living centers.

2. Talking. Some Christians have a unique gift of gab. Use your talent and read or tell Biblical stories to children, teach a Sunday School class, or lead a Bible study. Perhaps explore avenues to host a Christian-based radio talk show. Use your verbal skills to strike up some dialogue with those you meet and look for opportunities to work the message of Christ into the conversation.

3. Writing. Pick up your pen (or your laptop) and begin an inspirational blog or do some freelancing for Christian magazines, devotionals, and other publications. This is a wonderful way to spread the gospel. Research Christian writer conferences and network with Christians in the field to find out about additional opportunities.

4. Acting. If you love the performing arts, find a church that specializes in religious drama or plays and get involved. Or work with your church board or choir leader to start up a production department in your own church and look for scripts based on God's Word to help celebrate special occasions. You might ask God to help you write a play of your own or to help you find someone in the church who possesses this hidden talent. A church in my local region used to put on three huge productions each year for Easter, Independence Day, and Christmas, and these were attended by thousands of area residents

Develop Your Skills and Talents 141

who always looked forward to these events. This was a great way for the church to expand its ministry and spread the plan of salvation throughout the community. In addition, a couple from my church hosts a production each year before Halloween at a former salt mine. Dubbed the "Cavern of Choices," there are "demon guides" who tour the many visitors through the caves as various scenes depict right and wrong life choices along with the eternal consequences of each. Many visitors have accepted Christ at this annual event.

5. Driving. Some people love to get behind the wheel. Let your church leaders know you are available to drive the bus to transport senior citizens, handicapped, and underprivileged folks to the services. You might also volunteer to drive the youth or other groups on special trips. Some men from my church help drive our pastors when they speak at out-of-town meetings or conferences, and this is another way you might be able to assist.

6. Cooking. This is a good one. If your love is the kitchen, then spread it around and bake some cookies or a hot meal and take them to an elderly couple or to someone who is ill. Drop off some baked goods at the local hospice, homeless shelter, or other organization that helps the down-and-out. If your church provides bereavement dinners for families, this is a great way to use your culinary skills to offer comfort to others when they are in sorrow. You might also prepare dinners for visiting evangelists.

7. Hosting. If you like to entertain, then open your home to host a regular Bible study or an event for your Sunday School class. You might also volunteer to provide a room for a guest minister so he does not have to stay in a hotel. If your home is empty and you want a real challenge, consider foster care. There are many foster children in need of a place to stay, and you might provide temporary shelter until permanent homes can be found.
8. Building. Perhaps your talent is construction or other skilled craft. You can use your expertise on mission trips since many of these are organized to help build or repair churches, schools, and other structures in third-world countries. You can also use your skills locally and volunteer with organizations like Habitat for Humanity. Some missionary groups also travel to poor rural areas and inner cities of the US to help make improvements. You might also travel with a missionary team to provide storm relief to an area battered and damaged by hurricanes or other significant weather events.
9. Promoting. Some love to use marketing skills in their job. Why not use your education and experience to promote local church events in your area? Perhaps you could produce local appearances by prominent gospel artists, authors, and speakers. You may perhaps use your talents to help support your home church with advertisements, social media, and the weekly bulletin.

These are just a few examples, but you need to find the gift God has given you and expand on it to glorify the Lord. A. J. Green developed his talent of juggling to become a possible future Hall of Fame wide receiver. You won't know the extent of your talents until you begin to use them. Who Dey!

Week 39

WHAT DOES *WHO DEY* REALLY MEAN?

All Scripture is God-breathed and is useful for teaching, rebuking, correcting and training in righteousness.
—2 Timothy 3:16

What is the true meaning of *Who Dey*? I looked in the dictionary, but it's not there. When I do a search on Webster's website, I get such suggestions as *hidey, who'd, whoaed* and *whoever*.

Per a 2015 article on the subject by the *Cincinnati Enquirer*, it serves as an adjective, noun, pronoun, verb, adverb, a Malayan tiger at the Cincinnati Zoo, and even a beer. Bengals fans include it in a longer phrase they quote often: "Who dey, who dey, who dey think gonna beat dem Bengals?"

The motto is a victory chant, a cry of celebration, a term of endearment, and a way for devotees to communicate their solidarity. The slogan has appeared on shirts, signs, and even in the lights of the Cincinnati skyline.

There are multiple disagreements about the origination of the catchphrase, but one thing is for certain. Who Dey is a culture, a heritage, a way of life, a movement, a representation of a working-class town that bonds together once a week throughout the football season without any concerns about the use of proper grammar—it is a symbol of unity and gives the city its own personal brand. It's an identity.

Does your light shine for God and help you bond with fellow believers to show the world the joy of serving Christ?

For you have been born again, not of perishable seed, but of imperishable, through the living and enduring word of God.
—1 Peter 1:23

Huddle Up

Do your best to represent heaven's brand and be the best Christian you can be for the Lord. Do your words and actions express your devotion to Him?

Quick Snap

Make sure the world labels you a solid Bible-believing follower of God. Establish goals you want to achieve, and reach them in the most ethical way possible. Cheer on the other disciples on your team, and be a true ambassador of the Christian faith with these guidelines:

1. Have a moral foundation. "But to you who are listening I say, 'Love your enemies, do good to those who hate you, bless those who curse you, pray for those who mistreat you'" (Luke 6:27–28).
2. Put yourself last. "Do nothing out of selfish ambition or vain conceit. Rather, in humility value others above yourselves" (Philippians 2:3).

3. Resist temptation. "And lead us not into temptation, but deliver us from the evil one" (Matthew 6:13).
4. Be positive. "For the Lord takes delight in his people; he crowns the humble with victory" (Psalm 149:4).
5. Be accountable. "So then, each of us will give an account of ourselves to God" (Romans 14:12).
6. Keep good company. "The righteous choose their friends carefully, but the way of the wicked leads them astray" (Proverbs 12:26).
7. Be active in your community. "Honor the Lord with your wealth, with the firstfruits of all your crops" (Proverbs 3:9).
8. Take your family to church. "Start children off on the way they should go, and even when they are old they will not turn from it" (Proverbs 22:6).
9. Respect your spouse. "Husbands, in the same way be considerate as you live with your wives, and treat them with respect as the weaker partner and as heirs with you of the gracious gift of life, so that nothing will hinder your prayers" (1 Peter 3:7).
10. Praise and honor the Lord. "Let everything that has breath praise the Lord. Praise the Lord" (Psalm 150:6).

Accept God's call and strive to meet the expectations God sets before you. Submit to His plan for your life.

For God so loved the world that he gave his one and only Son, that whoever believes in him shall not perish but have eternal life.
—John 3:16

Who Dey!

Week 40

KEEP A SONG IN YOUR HEART

Speaking to one another with psalms, hymns, and songs from the Spirit. Sing and make music from your heart to the Lord.
—Ephesians 5:19

George Bird wrote the "Bengals Growl" while he was a patient in the hospital.

When his good friend, Paul Brown, was with the Cleveland Browns, he asked Bird to be the team's entertainment director. He organized a small band and performed at the home games. He followed Brown to Cincinnati and soon wrote the popular fight song that is now a home crowd favorite. Here are the words all Bengal fans know by heart:

> Hear that Bengal growlin' mean and angry
> Here he comes a prowlin' lean and hungry
> An offensive brute
> Run, pass, or boot
> And defensively he's rough, tough
> Cincinnati Bengals
> That's the team we're going to cheer to victory

> Touchdown Bengals get some points upon that board
> And win a game for Cincinnati.

The song is short and catchy and symbolizes the tone of the franchise. Fans sing along with the jingle and it helps to put them in the mood for a Sunday afternoon ball game.

Do you have a song in your heart? Does your excitement spill over to others?

> *Come, let us sing for joy to the Lord; let us shout aloud to the Rock of our salvation.*
>
> —Psalm 95:1

Huddle Up

When you have the joy of the Lord deep in your soul, you have a peace that is worth singing about. "You will go out in joy and be led forth in peace; the mountains and hills will burst into song before you, and all the trees of the field will clap their hands" (Isaiah 55:12).

Quick Snap

Pick one of your favorite Christian songs and commit it to memory. A song can signify a great milestone; it can help you rejoice or comfort and help you through a troubled time. Find a tune with lyrics that uplift, inspire, and speak to you. The song can be an old-time great or a new contemporary one. Here is an example of a treasured hymn that has been sung down through the ages:

> Blessed assurance, Jesus is mine!
> Oh, what a foretaste of glory divine!
> Heir of salvation, purchase of God,
> born of his Spirit, washed in his blood.
>
> This is my story, this is my song,
> praising my Savior all the day long.
> This is my story, this is my song,
> praising my Savior all the day long.
>
> Perfect communion, perfect delight,
> visions of rapture now burst on my sight.
> Angels descending bring from above
> echoes of mercy, whispers of love.
>
> Perfect submission, all is at rest.
> I in my Savior am happy and bless'd,
> watching and waiting, looking above,
> filled with his goodness, lost in his love.

When you have a song in your heart, the Spirit of the Lord shines around you. People know you are happy and might even ask why. Then you can share the *Amazing Grace* of Christ. When you have a sweet melody within your soul, no one can defeat you. Who Dey!

Week 41

JUST RUN FASTER

Let him turn away from evil and do good; let him seek peace and pursue it.

—1 Peter 3:11 ESV

The outlook was grim for the Orange and Black faithful. The Baltimore Ravens were about to score a touchdown to beat the Bengals in the NFL Wild-Card playoff game on January 15, 2023, at The Jungle.

The game was tied 17-17 and the Ravens had the ball at the Bengals' two-yard line in the final quarter with the clock ticking down. Cincinnati's defense had made plays all season long. But the odds were against them at this moment. Hope was fading.

Baltimore quarterback Tyler Huntley took the snap on a QB sneak and tried to jump over the pile of Ravens and Bengals fighting at the line of scrimmage. Bengals linebacker Logan Wilson managed to get his paw on the ball and knocked it in the air and it fell into the hands of defensive end Sam Hubbard.

The Cincinnati native was right where he was supposed to be at that moment. Hubbard, an Ohio boy through and through, instinctively darted for the end zone ninety-eight yards away. The 6-5, 265-pounder took off like a bolt of lightning. He rumbled ninety-eight-yards to give the Bengals an incredible 24-17 win to advance to the next round of the playoffs.

For Hubbard, it was a magnificent moment. He was born in Cincinnati and played college at The Ohio State University. In 2018, he was drafted in the third round by his home-team Bengals.

According to CBS Sports, the ninety-eight-yard fumble recovery for the TD was the longest fumble return touchdown in the history of the NFL playoffs and the longest go-ahead touchdown in the fourth in playoff history. The big guy was clocked by Next Gen Stats at a top speed of 17.43 mph.

When Bengals quarterback Joe Burrow was asked what was running through his mind when he saw Hubbard dashing down the middle of the field with the football and with several Ravens on his heels, he said, "I was thinking, *Just run fast, Sam, run faster.*"

Hubbard made it to the end zone for the amazing win. And that same football that Hubbard carried ninety-eight yards on that record-setting play now sits in Canton, Ohio, at the Pro Football Hall of Fame.

Sam snagged the ball out of the air and just ran as fast as he could.

But the one who endures to the end will be saved.
—Matthew 24:13 ESV

Huddle Up

Have you faced defeat in the face? Have you been on defense and felt like the devil was about to win and knock you out of contention? Did you even wonder if you could come through with a big play even with all of life's pressures on you?

Quick Snap

There are many times in life when you just have to dig in and look the devil in the eye and tell him that he is no match for the Lord. You cannot win the game by yourself. You must be ready to let God knock the ball out of the hands of devils and let it fall into your open arms. Then, just run. Here are some tips on how to flee evil:

1. Be aware. Sam Hubbard was ready to make the big play. You must have the same attitude and awareness. Just when you think all hope is lost, God can cause the other team to fumble. You can be aware of your surroundings by staying in the Word of God on a regular basis and by praying to the Lord every day. Ask Him to prepare your heart. Be ready to catch the ball and run.
2. Never challenge the enemy. Don't pick a fight with the devil, but at the same time don't back down. You are no match for the forces of evil alone. You must learn to draw the power, and even the desire, to resist sin from Jesus Christ. If you seek out the struggle, you will fail. Commune with God, be on guard, be

humble—do all of these things! But do not rely on those to win the battle. Instead, allow the Holy Spirit to intervene, and rely on Christ to cause the turnover,
3. Be humble. When you are humble in Christ, you are neither drawn in by Satan's lies, nor are you terrified by his threats. God will deliver you if you have a humble heart. "The fear of the Lord is hatred of evil. Pride and arrogance and the way of evil and perverted speech I hate" (Proverbs 8:13 ESV).
4. Resist and run: When the devil makes a blitz for your soul, take off and flee. Don't have the attitude that you will dabble in a little bit of sin. That won't work and he will take advantage of your weaknesses. Know what makes you weak and turn it over to the Lord. Then when the devil uses that weakness to lure you into his trap, that is when you call on Christ for strength and power, and then you run away. God promises that you can resist temptation, but it becomes harder when you begin to dabble in what tempts you. Eventually, you will give in. Just run away. "Submit yourselves therefore to God. Resist the devil, and he will flee from you" (James 4:7 ESV).

There are many more things you can do to battle the devil. You can pray more and surround yourself with like-minded friends who can help you when you struggle. You can occupy your time by volunteering or going to camp meetings and by worshiping God.

But the best thing you can do is what Sam Hubbard did best—just run. Who Dey!

Week 42

SET THE RECORD

For from his fullness we have all received, grace upon grace.
—John 1:16 ESV

Cincinnati running back Joe Mixon needed a big day. His Bengals were coming off from a horrendous Monday night loss at AFC North rival Cleveland the previous week.

But on November 6, 2022, Mixon made sure the Who Dey faithful cheered louder for the Orange and Black than ever before. Mixon scored a Bengals-record five touchdowns in a lopsided 42-21 win over the Carolina Panthers at The Jungle. The win boosted Cincinnati to 5-4 and resurrected the season that could have gone south.

Mixon rumbled for 153 yards on twenty-two attempts (7.0 yards-per-carry) and four touchdowns. He also had four receptions for fifty-eight yards and another score.

His five touchdowns were the most in team history.

After the game, he said the win was a great overall team performance and added he was happy to do his part for the club. "To come out here today and have a complete game and pass protection when my number was called, and then deliver for my teammates, (Joe) Burrow and the receivers, and be able to hit the right holes and do all the things to have a complete game, bro, I mean you can't ask for much better," Mixon told the media.

Mixon became the first NFL player with one-hundred-fifty-plus yards and four or more touchdowns from scrimmage in the first half of a game since Shaun Alexander did it for the Seahawks in week 4 of the 2002 season.

It was a big day in the Queen city for Mixon, who helped his team bounce back from a sloppy performance just six days prior.

For it is God who works in you, both to will and to work for his good pleasure.

—Philippians 2:13 ESV

Huddle Up

How have you responded to a bad week? Did you run and hide, or did you put in extra time and energy and redeem any lousy performances? Maybe you spouted off at your spouse or said something to a coworker that caused regret and shame. Or maybe you did something wrong and need to make it right.

Quick Snap

The best thing to do in any cases where you have overstepped your bounds is to make an immediate amends. The sooner this happens the better any relationship will be. Here are some ways to set the record and make things right when you are wrong:

1. Repent. First, ask God for forgiveness. Even though you are aware that He will forgive, go to Him, and ask with a humble heart. "Repent therefore, and turn back, that your sins may be blotted out" (Acts 3:19 ESV).
2. Admit it. Own up to your mistakes. Everyone has them, yet there are some who won't admit to their shortcomings. Be a bigger person and own up to what you did wrong.
3. No excuses. Under no circumstances utter the words "but" or "this is why I did what I did" or "the thing is" after the words I'm sorry. Those word negate any apology. Just say you are sorry for what you did or said. That puts the task for forgiveness on the other person.
4. Show humility. This is not the time to be bold or arrogant. True humbleness is stronger than any confidence. "When pride comes, then comes disgrace, but with the humble is wisdom" (Proverbs 11:2 ESV).
5. Be determined to do better. Mixon bounced back from a lousy game the week before and set a team record. You can do the same. Be determined to do better each week and each day. Break your own record of being nice.

If you don't admit to your mistakes and aim to grow as a person and a believer, you will stay in the same condition and become mean and bitter. When you acknowledge your weakness and shortcomings and improve, then you become stronger and closer to the Lord. Who Dey!

Week 43

THE PHANTOM CALL

For all that is secret will eventually be brought into the open, and everything that is concealed will be brought to light and made known to all.
—Luke 8:17 NLT

Cincinnati was less than two minutes away from winning Super Bowl LVI. The Los Angeles Rams were closing in on the end zone and had a crucial third-down play in the red zone. The Bengals needed a stop to hold on to their 20-16 lead. A field goal would not help LA—they needed a touchdown.

Rams QB Matthew Stafford was under pressure and flipped the ball to Cooper Kupp on third-and-eight. Bengals linebacker Logan Wilson batted the ball down and the Who Dey faithful cheered and thought they had the Rams where they wanted them. But a yellow flag fluttered onto the turf at SoFi Stadium and Wilson was called for a holding penalty, which gave the Rams an automatic first down.

Los Angeles would go on to score a touchdown and win the biggest game of the year 23-20 on February 13, 2022. But to all Bengals fans and many football analysts, the call should not have been made. NBC's Cris Collinsworth said, "That's what they called? Wow. In a game where there have not been that many ticky-tack fouls that was close."

And respected replay official and retired NFL referee Mike Pereira said, "Wilson gets called for holding. It's just not holding." Nevertheless, the penalty was called and mired the outcome of a great game.

Wilson knew deep down he did not commit the foul that led to the Rams getting another set of downs near the goal line and ultimately winning the Super Bowl. He's lived with it and has put it past him. He knows, as does anyone who knows anything about football, that it was not holding.

Have you ever been accused of something you did not do? Has it affected your spiritual walk with God and has it made you bitter?

> *So stop telling lies. Let us tell our neighbors the truth, for we are all parts of the same body.*
> —Ephesians 4:25 NLT

Huddle Up

You can't defend a lie or a bad call. Whenever you see people in a family setting or at church or in business, you will find mistruths. Has this ever happened to you? Gossip is a terrible tool used by the devil.

Quick Snap

There is not a whole lot you can do when someone has told a lie about you. It can cause damage you never knew existed. But you cannot let it bring you down. Here are some ways to cope with lies and the phantom call that might cost you the Super Bowl:

1. Pray for those who falsely accused you. This will be difficult, but remember Christ forgave on the Cross. "But I say, love your enemies! Pray for those who persecute you!" (Matthew 5:44 NLT).
2. Let the bitterness go. If you fail in this area, you will become as stone, and you won't have any compassion. And that is what you need to demonstrate the most.
3. Remind yourself that God will vindicate. As bad as you want to strike back, resist that human urge and turn it over to God. "Dear friends, never take revenge. Leave that to the righteous anger of God. For the Scriptures say, 'I will take revenge; I will pay them back,' says the Lord" (Romans 12:19 NLT).
4. Stay the course. Never give your haters the satisfaction of seeing you fail.
5. Keep your head up. Remind yourself through reading the Word of God that He loves you enough that He gave His life for *you*.

Wilson and the Bengals were dealt a tough blow at a crucial time in the biggest game of the year. No matter how much they could have protested, the call would not have been reversed. The same goes for you. If a lie is told on you, keep playing hard and keep playing fair and by the rules. You might lose a game, but you will be a winner in life. Who Dey!

Week 44

REUNITED

In my Father's house are many mansions: if it were not so, I would have told you. I go to prepare a place for you.
—John 14:2 KJV

No matter your age, most NFL fans remember the greatest quarterback/wide receiver combinations of all time.

- Steve Young and Jerry Rice
- Terry Bradshaw and Lynn Swann
- Roger Staubach and Drew Pearson
- Troy Aikman and Michael Irvin
- Kurt Warner and Isaac Bruce
- Tom Brady and Julian Edelman

Now you can add Joe Burrow and Ja'Marr Chase to that list of greatness. The dynamic duo of Burrow and Chase is just plain exciting. The two have been linked since their championship days at Louisiana State University when they teamed up to lead the Tigers to the College Football Playoffs National Championship in 2019.

Following that year at LSU, Burrow was the number-one pick in the NFL Draft and the Bengals snagged the Ohio native. But Chase, who had another year at LSU, opted out of the 2020 campaign to focus on his NFL Draft stock.

Every NFL expert said that the Bengals needed to draft an offensive lineman, especially after Burrow went down with a serious knee injury. But Burrow, the 2021 NFL comeback player of the year, lobbied hard for his former college teammate and the Bengals brass listened and selected Chase as their first-round pick. The Unanimous All-American was the fifth overall selection in the draft.

And the combo has been electric ever since. They know each other's moves and thoughts and have piled up the TDs and team records. They seem to read each other's minds on the field.

Chase was named the NFL Offensive Rookie of the Year in 2021 and they led the Bengals to Super Bowl LVI. Burrow has rewritten nearly every Bengals offensive record. Together, they are unstoppable most of the time.

The future is bright for the two great players. They were reunited and all the Queen City was happy. You, too, as a Bengal Believer, will be reunited with your loved ones who left a testimony of faith. That's exciting too.

For our conversation is in heaven; from whence also we look for the Saviour, the Lord Jesus Christ.
—Philippians 3:20 KJV

Huddle Up

Who do you miss on earth? Who do you want to be reunited with in heaven? Are you sure your sins are forgiven? Are you on the team roster to pass through the gates of pearl?

Quick Snap

These are serious questions you must ask yourself on a regular basis. Is there anything keeping you from reaching the streets of gold? Here are some reasons to make heaven your ultimate goal and make sure you are headed that way.

1. Heaven is a place built for worship. Just think of your favorite NFL stadium and how excited you become the day before you head to the big game. Do you have this same excitement for heaven? "But ye are come unto Mount Sion, and unto the city of the living God, the heavenly Jerusalem, and to an innumerable company of angel" (Hebrews 12:22 KJV).
2. All nations will praise God forever. Just think about how happy you are when your team wins a big game. You will rejoice with the Lord in heaven. "After this I beheld, and, lo, a great multitude, which no man could number, of all nations, and kindreds, and people, and tongues, stood before the throne, and before the Lamb, clothed with white robes, and palms in their hands; And cried with a loud voice, saying, Salvation to our God which sitteth upon the throne, and unto the Lamb" (Revelation 7:9–10 KJV).

3. Heaven will have gates of pearl and streets of gold. This will just be awesome!
4. God is the eternal light. In heaven, you will praise the Lord in the highest. "And there shall be no night there; and they need no candle, neither light of the sun; for the Lord God giveth them light: and they shall reign for ever and ever" (Revelation 22:5 KJV).
5. The reunion of your loved ones. This will be amazing. "Then we which are alive and remain shall be caught up together with them in the clouds, to meet the Lord in the air: and so shall we ever be with the Lord" (1 Thessalonians 4:17 KJV).

And this list can go on and on. But the main reason to go to heaven is to be with the One who died for you. Who Dey!

Week 45

DO YOUR BEST, NO MATTER THE OUTCOME

Show yourself in all respects to be a model of good works, and in your teaching show integrity, dignity.
—Titus 2:7 ESV

Not many players in the NFL enjoyed a rookie season like Bengals kicker Evan McPherson did. As a fifth-round draft pick out of Florida, he quickly became one of the top kickers in the league as well as a fan favorite in Cincinnati.

He earned the nickname "Money Mac" because he produced in the clutch. In his rookie season in 2021, McPherson made five game-winning walk-off field goals as time expired—and that included two in the playoffs.

"Money Mac" was good on twelve field goals from fifty-plus yards in both the regular and postseason combined, and tied for the most field goals made in the playoffs (fourteen) with legendary kicker Adam Vinatieri.

On November 21, he tied an NFL record by nailing three field goals from over fifty yards in one game and went four-for-four in the Bengals' 32-13 Wild Card win over the Las Vegas Raiders. The win was the first playoff victory for the franchise in thirty-one years. In the next round, McPherson's foot gave Cincinnati a 19-16 win over favored Tennessee, which sent them to the AFC Championship game.

Against the Chiefs, he was four-for-four, including the game-winner and the 27-24 win in Kansas City that sent the Bengals to Super Bowl LVI. He quietly boasted a spectacular rookie season and was not even considered for Rookie of the Year honors. For many, this was a major snub. Have you ever felt snubbed by the world or by your friends?

> *And let us not grow weary of doing good, for in due season we will reap, if we do not give up.*
>
> —Galatians 6:9 ESV

Huddle Up

Maybe you have felt overlooked. This is not uncommon, but that doesn't make it any better. Perhaps you have done all you can and still did not receive that promotion. Or maybe you feel like you've been erased from people who you thought cared about you.

Quick Snap

People can be cruel and hold grudges. But never let that stop you from being the best you that you can be. Here are some tips to stay strong and to keep going, even when you feel overlooked or underappreciated:

1. Distance yourself from worldliness. Sometimes you can get lost in what you are doing in the workplace or in the world. You need a refresher and that comes about with distance. Things of the world can cause a divide between you and your heavenly Father. Put some distance between your problems.
2. Pray and fast. One of the first steps to becoming a better Christian is to get away from temptations and sin. When you commit to fasting and prayer, your soul will be renewed with a stronger desire to serve.
3. Serve others. This will allow you to see the struggles of other people, and it will help you to put your own life in perspective. "In all toil there is profit, but mere talk tends only to poverty" (Proverbs 14:23 ESV).
4. Find like-minded people. If those who hurt you don't share the same beliefs that you do, maybe it's time to find new friends. Pray about this and consider a change in your circle.
5. Take a break. Sometimes the best thing you can do for yourself is get away for a bit. This is not "running away from your problems" but simply allowing yourself to experience something new and a refresher. Take a long weekend or go on a mission trip to help others. This will do wonders.
6. Stay committed to the Word. There will be moments when you do not understand why you are going through a struggle but find comfort in the Bible and don't negotiate with God. "And let us not grow weary of doing good, for in due season we will reap, if we do not give up" (Galatians 6:9 ESV).

Money Mac did not get the praise he deserved from the NFL for his unwavering performance his rookie year, but he knew he was appreciated by his fans and teammates. And there might be times when you feel snubbed by the world. But when you consider the fact that God loves you and will always be there for you, it is enough for you to give it your best, no matter the outcome. Who Dey!

Week 46

NO REFUND NEEDED

If you openly declare that Jesus is Lord and believe in your heart that God raised him from the dead, you will be saved. For it is by believing in your heart that you are made right with God, and it is by openly declaring your faith that you are saved.

—Romans 10:9–10 NLT

The game was all set—except no one in the NFL told the Bengals. Cincinnati stormed into Buffalo on January 22, 2023, in the AFC Divisional Championship game in the snow to take on the Bills.

The NFL brass was obviously counting on a Bills victory in hopes of a big rematch against Buffalo and the Kansas City Chiefs. They anticipated this so much that the league had already announced a neutral location for the game and put game tickets on sale—*before* the Bengals even played the game.

More than fifty thousand tickets for the possible Chiefs/Bills game were sold and the stadium in Atlanta was getting prepared for the AFC Championship game between Buffalo and Kansas City. But Cincinnati had something else in mind. Quarterback Joe Burrow threw two touchdown passes and the Bengals defense swarmed and harassed Buffalo QB Josh Allen in a 27-10 lopsided Cincy win.

The Bengals—and not the Bills—were going to face the Chiefs in the AFC Championship rematch. After the win, Burrow had a tongue-in-cheek response to the NFL: "Better send those refunds," he said.

To all Believers in Christ . . . no refund is needed.

For the grace of God has been revealed, bringing salvation to all people. And we are instructed to turn from godless living and sinful pleasures. We should live in this evil world with wisdom, righteousness, and devotion to God.
—Titus 2:11–12 NLT

Huddle Up

Once you give your life to the Lord and decide to live as a follower, your name is written down in the Lamb's Book of Life. Your debt has been paid and there is no refund needed, if you stay in God's good grace.

Quick Snap

Living the life of a Christian is the best life you can imagine. You will have no desire to turn away from Him. But the devil will have other plans. Here are some ways to stay strong in your faith:

1. Show up. No coach will ever put a player in the lineup if that athlete never comes to practice. Why should he? The player will have no clue what to do and will put the team at risk of a loss. The same applies to you. If you don't go to church or Sunday school or a Bible study on a regular basis, you will not be in the shape God wants for you.
2. Stand up. Worship God in all ways and all times. Praise the Lord in good and difficult times. "For God is Spirit, so those who worship him must worship in spirit and in truth" (John 4:24 NLT).
3. Kneel. Pray and talk to the Lord daily. The key to winning a divisional playoff game is communication. The same goes for you and your relationship with Christ. Kneel. Thank Him. Be grateful. Ask in humility and praise His name in advance. "But when you pray, go away by yourself, shut the door behind you, and pray to your Father in private. Then your Father, who sees everything, will reward you" (Matthew 6:6 NLT).
4. Be true to the Bible. A player cannot be effective if he does not read and know the playbook. You as a Christian must know God's instruction booklet for you. Read it. Read it again. Then read it again.
5. Live with integrity. Do what is right. Don't embarrass the Lord with your testimony.

Bengal players and fans felt disrespected when the NFL put Cincinnati out of contention before a game was even played. The team responded and knocked out the Bills in

Buffalo and sent a message that they were to be taken as a serious contender. The NFL was forced to send out thousands of dollars in refunds and had to wipe the egg off their face. When you accept Jesus Christ as your Savior, you'll never have to worry about Him losing or turning His back on you. Who Dey!

Week 47

THE COMEBACK

"For My thoughts are not your thoughts, Nor are your ways My ways," says the LORD.

—Isaiah 55:8 NKJV

Week 11 in 2020 was a bad day for Bengals QB Joe Burrow and for the faithful followers of the team. In a game against Washington on November 20, the standout QB suffered a torn left ACL and MCL and was carted off the field. Cincinnati finished the season 4-11-1. Bengal believers were stunned and shocked.

A few years prior, in the 2005 NFL Wild Card Playoff game, they watched in horror when quarterback Carson Palmer went down in a playoff game against Pittsburgh with a similar injury. He was never quite the same quarterback after that.

But Joe was different. After reconstructive surgery and rehab, the number-one pick in the NFL Draft was ready to make a comeback. The next season, the college football Heisman Trophy winner lit up the field and led the Bengals to a 10-7 overall record—which was more wins than the two previous seasons combined.

Cincinnati earned its first AFC North title since 2015 and made its first appearance in a Super Bowl since 1988. Burrow led the NFL in completion percentage (70.4) and yards per attempt (8.9). The Louisiana State University product threw for a franchise high with 4,611 yards passing and thirty-four touchdowns.

He became the second Bengal to win Comeback Player of the Year honors, joining Jon Kitna when he won the award in 2002.

What a comeback indeed.

For as the heavens are higher than the earth, So are My ways higher than your ways, And My thoughts than your thoughts.

—Isaiah 55:9 NKJV

Huddle Up

Have you been injured as a follower of Christ? Was there a time when a person you trusted did something to hurt you, or told lies about you to others? Maybe you were wronged by a church leader or a member of your family. No matter what happened or who did it, you may have used that circumstance to drift away from God in your spiritual journey.

Quick Snap

People do stumble and make mistakes that can lead to emotional or spiritual hurt. Joe came back from a serious knee injury and led the Bengals to an appearance in Super Bowl LVI the next season. He didn't give up and neither should you.

Here are some tips to consider when you must battle back from an injury caused within your community:

1. Realize there is purpose in the pain. No one wants to be a martyr and you should never take advantage of or manipulate others because of your pain. It's OK to ask "why?" But it's just as important to understand and trust God for all that is taking place. Joe came back stronger than ever. And so can you. Use your experience to help others.
2. Reject the lie that God doesn't care. You may feel alone but be assured God is with you. Go read the poem "Footprints in the Sand" and understand the Lord will carry you through the darkest times.
3. Realize your identity. God made you in His image. You are a child of the King and don't let Satan tell you any different. "But as many as received Him, to them He gave the right to become children of God, to those who believe in His name" (John 1:12 NKJV).
4. Recognize unconditional love. When someone puts conditions on their "love" for you, that is pure manipulation. God loves you without conditions.
5. Praise your way through the pain. Give God glory no matter what you go through. You will find your strength and determination will increase and grow stronger. "I will praise you, O Lord, with my whole heart; I will tell of all Your marvelous works" (Psalm 9:1 NKJV).
6. Invest in others. Put aside your needs and give back. Through this, you will understand everyone goes through battles. Help someone through theirs.

The devil wants you on the bench or in the locker room. Don't let the lies he tells keep you from serving God. If you have drifted, you can come back to Him. And the best part is that after you seek the Lord and ask for His forgiveness, He *will* take you back. Make the comeback! Who Dey!

Week 48

GOD CHOSE YOU

The LORD your God is in your midst, a mighty one who will save; he will rejoice over you with gladness; he will quiet you by his love; he will exult over you with loud singing.
—Zephaniah 3:17 ESV

On April 23, 2020, in Paradise, Nevada, the Cincinnati Bengals had the first pick in the NFL Draft.

There was no drama. No surprises. No last minute deals. They wanted Louisiana State University quarterback Joe Burrow and they got him. He was touted as a cool, collected QB who could stand pressure and win ball games. Football ran in his blood and family as his father was drafted by the Green Bay Packers in 1976. Jimmy Burrow went on to play in the Canadian Football League before going into coaching football at the college level.

Joe Burrow played high school football at The Plains, a small town near Athens, Ohio, and was recruited and committed to play for The Ohio State University Buckeyes in 2014. After things did not work out as planned at OSU, he transferred to LSU in 2018.

What a great move.

As a junior he led the Tigers to a 10-3 record and a win over UCF in the Fiesta Bowl. He finished the year by completing 219 of 379 passes for 2,894 yards, sixteen touchdowns, and five interceptions. He also rushed for 399 yards and seven touchdowns off 128 carries.

The next year, he compiled 5,671 yards passing and set an FBS single-season record with sixty touchdowns and earned the prestigious Heisman Trophy. But the topper was the College National Championship win over Clemson. He was a unanimous All-American and won the Walter Camp Award, the Johnny Unitas Golden Arm Award, the Davey O'Brien Award, and the Manning Award, to name a few.

Perhaps the most attractive characteristic above and beyond his talents was his confidence and ability to make his teammates better. Within three years, he led the Bengals to a Super Bowl appearance and a pair of AFC Championship games. He is a good fit for the Bengals, and the Cincinnati faithful love and have respect for him.

April 23, 2020, was a good day for Bengal Believers.

How much does God love you?

The steadfast love of the LORD never ceases; his mercies never come to an end; they are new every morning; great is your faithfulness.

—Lamentations 3:22–23 ESV

Huddle Up

Have you ever pondered God's love for you? Maybe there have been times in your life when you needed assurance that He loves you. Perhaps someone close to you betrayed you or circumstances in your life turned south.

Quick Snap

When you are physically alone or feel abandoned, you need to know the massive amount of love the Lord has for you. Here are some things to consider when you need to feel His adoration for you:

1. God's love for you is perfect. You can read all the books and devotionals you want, but you will never find a more perfect love than that of God's love for you. He sacrificed His son for you and will forgive you of your sins if you ask. "See what kind of love the Father has given to us, that we should be called children of God; and so we are. The reason why the world does not know us is that it did not know him" (1 John 3:1 ESV).
2. God's love for you is never-ending. No matter what you do, His love for you will never stop. He made you. He wants the best for you. But if you have done wrong, He will forgive you if you ask, but that doesn't mean your life will be without consequences. His love will get you through the tough times when others may leave. "Who shall separate us from the love of Christ? Shall tribulation, or distress, or persecution, or famine, or nakedness, or danger, or sword?" (Romans 8:35 ESV).
3. God's love for you is real. You want a love that is real. When you ask God into your life, you will feel His

love for you. You want a love that will last and will fulfill your needs. You found it with the Lord.
4. God's love for you is life-changing. When you experience God's love, you will have all you need. The searching will be over, and your life will change for the better. You will have a different outlook and you will have peace and joy, no matter your circumstances. "I have been crucified with Christ. It is no longer I who live, but Christ who lives in me. And the life I now live in the flesh I live by faith in the Son of God, who loved me and gave himself for me" (Galatians 2:20 ESV).

You are loved. God loves you. He chose you in the first round and you are precious in His sight. The fans in Cincinnati looked at Joe Burrow as the football savior of the town. He is loved and his talents are appreciated. God's love for you is even bigger than that. Who Dey!

Week 49

END THE STREAK AND GO TO THE SUPER BOWL

And it shall come to pass afterward, that I will pour out my Spirit on all flesh; your sons and your daughters shall prophesy, your old men shall dream dreams, and your young men shall see visions.

—Joel 2:28 ESV

The odds were against the Bengals, but they marched into Arrowhead Stadium on January 30, 2022, with a chance to go to the Super Bowl. Cincinnati fell behind by eighteen points and hope was beginning to fade for the Cincinnati faithful.

But Bengals quarterback Joe Burrow, who finished the game with two hundred fifty yards passing and completed twenty-three of thirty-eight passes with two TDs, made some key plays with his legs under pressure and engineered a game-winning drive. That drive was set up when Bengals defensive back Vonn Bell picked off a pass from KC QB Patrick Mahomes near midfield in overtime.

Cincinnati running back Joe Mixon plowed through the Chiefs' defense and gave Bengals rookie kicker Evan McPherson good field position to boot a thirty-one-yard AFC Championship-winning field goal in OT.

The win sent the Bengals to Super Bowl LVI, the team's first appearance in the big show since 1989, and stopped the Chiefs' bid to win a third-straight AFC Championship. "If you would have told me before the season that we'd be going to the Super Bowl, I probably would have called you crazy," Burrow said. "But then we played a whole season, and nothing surprises me now."

What a turnaround from previous seasons when the Bengals finished last in the AFC North. What bad streaks do you want to stop?

This God—his way is perfect; the word of the LORD proves true; he is a shield for all those who take refuge in him.
—Psalm 18:30 ESV

Huddle Up

You are human and will go through some bad times. You might finish last in your conference two years in a row, but that doesn't give you the right to lie down and quit. God is good in the bad time and joyous moments. Can you overcome a big deficit with a lot on the line?

Quick Snap

It won't be easy and there will be times of doubt and discouragement, but you can come up with the interception to set up a game-winner. Here are some things to avoid that might keep you on a losing skid:

1. Laziness. When you stop doing what you should to be a successful Christian, you become lazy. When you fail to do what is right, that is just as bad as doing wrong. When you know you need to read God's Word and you don't, that's laziness. When you stop praying and stop going to church, that invites the devil to come in and patronize you. "So whoever knows the right thing to do and fails to do it, for him it is sin" (James 4:17 ESV).
2. Indifference. This is when you fail to recognize the needs of others. When you fall into this area, you are being selfish and putting your needs first. "Finally, brothers, whatever is true, whatever is honorable, whatever is just, whatever is pure, whatever is lovely, whatever is commendable, if there is any excellence, if there is anything worthy of praise, think about these things" (Philippians 4:8 ESV).
3. Irresponsibility. This comes into play when you disobey God's plan for you. If you have children and they disobey your instructions, negative consequences might happen. The prodigal son found this out the hard way, but his father still loved him. "Therefore, be very strong to keep and to do all that is written in the Book of the Law of Moses, turning aside from it neither to the right hand nor to the left" (Joshua 23:6 ESV).
4. Habits. To keep going back to what got you into trouble is wrong. God will forgive you, but He

expects you to change your ways when you decide to follow Him.
5. Acceptance. Do not accept sin. You will make mistakes but you should have a goal to have high standards. Avoid what puts you in a compromising situation. For example: if you have a problem with alcohol, then stay away from bars and nightclubs. "For the wages of sin is death, but the free gift of God is eternal life in Christ Jesus our Lord" (Romans 6:23 ESV).

The Bengals did not accept the fact that the Chiefs had gone to two straight Super Bowls. Cincinnati had other plans and ended the streak. You can do the same when up against the odds. Who Dey!

Week 50

THE BALTIMORE BEATDOWN

If my people who are called by my name humble themselves, and pray and seek my face and turn from their wicked ways, then I will hear from heaven and will forgive their sin and heal their land.

—2 Chronicles 7:14 ESV

Some players in the NFL tend to open their mouths before a big game. Trash-talking is common and fans love it. But on rare occasions, a coach might get into the fray too.

Such was the case before the Bengals whipped up on the Baltimore Ravens before the December 26, 2021, week 16 AFC North contest.

Before the game, Ravens defensive coordinator Wink Martindale was asked about how the team was preparing to defend Bengals quarterback Joe Burrow and if they were prepared to play with the same tactics they used the prior week against Aaron Rodgers and the Green Bay Packers.

He said, "Aaron Rodgers is a Hall of Fame QB, and I don't think we're ready to buy a gold jacket for Joe (Burrow)."

The Bengals signal caller responded and broke Cincinnati's single-game record for passing yards set by Boomer Esiason, in the lopsided 41-21 divisional win, by throwing for 525 yards and four touchdowns.

Burrow accomplished this milestone by spreading the ball around to several of his wide receivers. Tee Higgins hauled in twelve catches for 194 yards and Ja'Marr Chase had seven receptions for 125 yards.

After the game, Burrow said the team was in perfect position. "We're right where we want to be," he said. "We knew the kind of team we had. You couldn't ask for a better situation right now. We control our destiny. Win these next two games, and we've got the division locked."

Are you where God wants you to be? Do you know His will for your life?

> *And he said to him, "You shall love the Lord your God with all your heart and with all your soul and with all your mind. This is the great and first commandment. And a second is like it: You shall love your neighbor as yourself. On these two commandments depend all the Law and the Prophets."*
>
> —Matthew 22:37–40 ESV

Huddle Up

You may know someone who has spent years trapped in an endless cycle of bad choices. Perhaps you are that person who has made wrong decisions. The book of Galatians tells you that a man will reap what he sows.

Quick Snap

Is your journey filled with potholes and sharp turns? Maybe you have come to a fork on the road and have indecision on which way to go. Do you want to follow the Lord's path, or your own road? How do you know the difference? Here are some ways to know the direction for your life from the Lord:

1. Commit your decision to God. This can only come by prayer and asking God for His will, and not your own. "Let the words of my mouth and the meditation of my heart be acceptable in your sight, O LORD, my rock and my redeemer" (Psalm 19:14 ESV).
2. Confirm your choices in Scripture. Search the Word of God for those who had similar circumstances. See how they handled it and what the results were. Read accounts from those who made good decisions and wrong ones too.
3. Be aware of your situation. Make sure what you want is not an emotional reaction. God will work through you *and* around you and your surroundings. Maybe God is navigating you through a circumstance.
4. Seek honest advice. Go to those who have been an inspiration to you over the years. Try not to seek advice from a "yes" person, but from someone who has been through it all and survived.
5. Turn it over to Jesus. Be quiet and listen to what God reveals to you. Step back and get out of the way and let Him work. "And your ears shall hear a word behind you, saying, 'This is the way, walk in it,' when

you turn to the right or when you turn to the left" (Isaiah 30:21 ESV).
6. 6. Praise Him and trust in the outcome. Once He has given you direction, don't hesitate. Do it. Go. But praise Him and thank Him for His goodness. Believe Him. Trust Him. Praise Him. The devil might try to discourage you, but that will only confirm it for you and give you added motivation. "Let them praise your great and awesome name! Holy is he!" (Psalm 99:3 ESV).

A coach said something before the game that inspired Joe Burrow. He came out and set a team record and led his team to a big win. You can do the same. Let God lead your path and make sure the devil watches as you set a personal record for spiritual victories. Who Dey!

Week 51

HAPPY BIRTHDAY

So, whether you eat or drink, or whatever you do, do all to the glory of God.
—1 Corinthians 10:31 ESV

Cincinnati defensive back Cam Taylor-Britt made a big impact on October 15, 2023, and helped the Bengals down visiting Seattle at The Jungle. The University of Nebraska product made a nifty play to knock down a pass from Seahawks quarterback Geno Smith that could have been a touchdown if not for Taylor-Britt's agility.

Then later in the game, he picked off a Smith pass on an acrobatic diving play to give the ball back to his offense. In the end, the Bengals won the game 17-13 thanks in part to two magnificent defensive plays.

He helped his team win, and it was also his birthday to boot. Taylor-Britt gave himself a gift with the pick. "I never had an interception on my birthday before," he said. "That was cool."

The celebration in the locker room after the game was because the team won a close game. But for Taylor-Britt, he contributed in a big way. For him to have made it to the highest level in football is a miracle.

When he was in the tenth and eleventh grades in high school, he had two major knee surgeries and other leg injuries. But his faith in God stayed strong and he kept studying the spiritual playbook. That's why he has "God's Child" tattooed on his leg, close to where he had surgery.

"I honestly thought I was done with football when I was in high school after that second surgery," he said. "So, when I say I'm God's child, I mean it. He would not have put me through that and not get me out of it. He might put some of His children through a lot of things, knowing that they can handle it. I know I am where I am today because of His love for me."

Are you God's child? Do you celebrate not only a birthday, but every day He allows you to breathe?

These things I have spoken to you, that my joy may be in you, and that your joy may be full.

—John 15:11 ESV

Huddle Up

You don't need a special occasion, like a birthday, to celebrate Christ's love for you. Have you considered being grateful and thankful daily? Do you only celebrate the resurrection of Christ on Easter, or His birth on Christmas?

Quick Snap

It's OK to celebrate your big day and holidays like Easter and Christmas. But those should not be the only times you honor God. How hard would it be to celebrate salvation and restoration each day? Sounds easy, right? Or is it? Here are some ways to celebrate God's love for you:

1. Show kindness every day. God showed grace and kindness to you when He forgave your sins. Do the same. "Be kind to one another, tenderhearted, forgiving one another, as God in Christ forgave you" (Ephesians 4:32 ESV).
2. Be thankful every day. Instead of focusing on what you don't have, look at what you possess. Then thank God for what He has allowed you to have.
3. Rise above negativity every day. The news and current events can drag you down. Your situations might also invite negative thoughts. Rise above that and let Christ lead you.
4. Recognize you have a purpose every day. God wants you to be happy. But you might go through struggles. Cam had two knee surgeries and doubted he would ever play football again. But God had plans. You do as well. "For God gave us a spirit not of fear but of power and love and self-control" (2 Timothy 1:7 ESV).
5. Read His Word and pray, every day. The Bible is not just a book—it's your inspiration and directions. Seek Him in prayer often.

6. Be a servant, every day. Humble yourself to the Lord and never take anyone for granted. "One's pride will bring him low, but he who is lowly in spirit will obtain honor" (Proverbs 29:23 ESV).

Your life today is a blessing and a gift. If you don't open the gift, it's your fault. Don't be too busy that you forget what Christ has done for you. Every day. Who Dey!

Week 52

GOD WILL GIVE YOU A SECOND CHANCE

Jesus answered him, "Truly, truly, I say to you, unless one is born again he cannot see the kingdom of God."
—John 3:3 ESV

The Cincinnati faithful were pumped. Monday Night Football was in the Queen City on January 2, 2022, and there was a lot on the line for the Bengals, including home field advantage in the NFL playoffs. But soon into the game, more than sixty-five thousand at Paul Brown Stadium were shocked and silenced.

During what appeared to be a routine play, Buffalo Bills defensive back Damar Hamlin collided with Cincinnati wide receiver Tee Higgins, fell to the turf, and went into cardiac arrest on the field.

Everyone was stunned when Damar's lifeless body fell to the ground early in the second quarter. Buffalo Bills medical staff rushed onto the field and administered cardiopulmonary resuscitation (CPR) and also used an automated external defibrillator (AED) before they transported Damar to a local hospital.

On the way to the hospital, he flatlined again, but God had other plans. This was evident especially after everyone on the field—both teams included—and the thousands seated in the stadium called out to the Lord for help. The 212th overall pick in the 2021 NFL Draft by the Bills survived.

The game was suspended and later canceled the same week. But that was not the main concern. The entire nation was gripped by the story and rejoiced as he continued to improve. Christians knew that God was in control while nonbelievers had to admit there was more than "luck" to Damar's recovery.

After the Bills defeated New England the week after Damar went down, Buffalo quarterback Josh Allen told the media in a press conference: "I was just going around to my teammates saying, 'God's real.' You can't draw that one up, write that one up any better."

The Bills organization posted a video of Damar's official Twitter account. It was the first time he had addressed his health scare on camera. "What happened to me on Monday Night Football, it was a direct example of God using me as a vessel to share my passion and my love directly from my heart with the entire world," he said. "Now, I'm able to give it back to kids and communities all across the world who need it the most and that's always been my dream, that's always been what I stood for and what I will continue to stand for."

After he thanked the trainers and medical staff, teammates, and fans for their support, he went on to give God the glory. "This is just the beginning of the impact I wanted to have on the world and with God's guidance, I will continue to do wonderful and great things," he added. "God is using me in a different way today."

God brought Damar back to life because He was not finished with him. And He wanted the entire world to take note of His mighty power. What better way than to show His might than on Monday Night Football?

God can give you a second chance at the best life ever.

Then came Peter to him, and said, Lord, how oft shall my brother sin against me, and I forgive him? till seven times? Jesus saith unto him, I say not unto thee, Until seven times: but, Until seventy times seven.

—Matthew 18:21–22 KJV

Huddle Up

Life is short. There is no time for bitterness, resentment, and discouragement. The devil wants you to be sidelined with these injuries. He also desires you to die. Satan wants to destroy you and everyone you love. Perhaps your story is not over but is hampered by unforgiveness and hatred. Forgiveness is a wonderful gift, until you are the one who must give it.

Quick Snap

God grants forgiveness when you ask. But He won't just give it to you. It must be asked. The hardest part about this is when you realize you must let go of your sin. Don't ask to take it away because you may still want to hold on to it a little. Give it to Him. Mistakes fester and brew in your mind and memory. Learn from them and move forward. Never return to your old ways but use the pain from the past to motivate you toward success. Here are some suggestions on how to make the most of your second chance:

1. Forgive others. After you have asked God to clean your slate and forgive you of your sins, you should do the same and grant forgiveness. Let go of the feelings the devil planted in your mind from those who may have hurt or offended you. "But if ye forgive not men their trespasses, neither will your Father forgive your trespasser" (Matthew 6:15 KJV).
2. Be grateful. God gave the life of His only Son so you can live in heaven. Never forget that. He paid the debt of your sin with His blood. "Wherefore we receiving a kingdom which cannot be moved, let us have grace, whereby we may serve God acceptably with reverence and godly fear" (Hebrews 12:28 KJV).
3. Stay focused. Once you have left the past in the locker room, move forward and be productive for the Lord.
4. Get involved. Attend church on a regular basis and be a part of a community and congregation. You matter and have a place. Pay your dues and be ready to play when you are put into the game.
5. Praise God always. God is, and has been, good to you. Your day may not go as planned, but as long as you have breath and wake up every day, praise His name for another opportunity. "For the Lord is great and greatly to be praised; He is to be feared above all gods" (Psalm 96:4 NKJV).

God gave Damar a second chance. And Damar said he knows the Lord has plans for him. He has the right attitude. Let's hope you don't have to stare death in the face to realize God has plans for you. But you must be willing to let Him guide you and give you the chance to praise and honor Him. Who Dey!

www.ingramcontent.com/pod-product-compliance
Lightning Source LLC
Chambersburg PA
CBHW070137080526
44586CB00015B/1738